Teaching Caribbean Poetry

Teaching Caribbean Poetry will inform and inspire readers with a love for, and understanding of, the dynamic world of Caribbean poetry. This unique volume sets out to enable secondary English teachers and their students to engage with a wide range of poetry, past and present; to understand how histories of the Caribbean underpin the poetry and relate to its interpretation; and to explore how Caribbean poetry connects with environmental issues.

Written by literary experts with extensive classroom experience, this lively and accessible book is immersed in classroom practice, and examines:

- popular aspects of Caribbean poetry, such as performance poetry;
- different forms of Caribbean language;
- the relationship between music and poetry;
- new voices, as well as well-known and distinguished poets, including John Agard (winner of the Queen's Medal for Poetry, 2012), Kamau Brathwaite, Lorna Goodison, Olive Senior and Derek Walcott;
- the crucial themes within Caribbean poetry such as inequality, injustice, racism, 'othering', hybridity, diaspora and migration;
- the place of Caribbean poetry on the GCSE/CSEC and CAPE syllabi, covering appropriate themes, poetic forms and poets for exam purposes.

Throughout this absorbing book, the authors aim to combat the widespread 'fear' of teaching poetry, enabling teachers to teach it with confidence and enthusiasm and helping students to experience the rewards of listening to, reading, interpreting, performing and writing Caribbean poetry.

Beverley Bryan is Professor of Language Education at the University of the West Indies' Mona School of Education, Jamaica, and a past Head of Department and Director of the School of Education.

Morag Styles is Professor of Children's Poetry at the University of Cambridge's Faculty of Education, and a Fellow of Homerton College, University of Cambridge, UK.

NATE

The National Association for the Teaching of English (NATE), founded in 1963, is the professional body for all teachers of English from primary to post-16. Through its regions, committees and conferences, the association draws on the work of classroom practitioners, advisers, consultants, teacher trainers, academics and researchers to promote dynamic and progressive approaches to the subject by means of debate, training and publications. NATE is a charity reliant on membership subscriptions. If you teach English in any capacity, please visit **www.nate.org.uk** and consider joining NATE, so the association can continue its work and give teachers of English and the subject a strong voice nationally.

This series of books co-published with NATE reflects the organisation's dedication to promoting standards of excellence in the teaching of English, from early years through to university level. Titles in this series promote innovative and original ideas that have practical classroom outcomes and support teachers' own professional development.

Books in the NATE series include both pupil and classroom resources and academic research aimed at English teachers, students on PGCE/ITT courses and NQTs.

Titles in this series include:

International Perspectives on Teaching English in a Globalised World
Edited by Andrew Goodwyn, Louann Reid and Cal Durrant

Teaching English Language 16–19
Martin Illingworth and Nick Hall

Unlocking Poetry (CD-ROM)
Trevor Millum and Chris Warren

Teaching English Literature 16–19
Carol Atherton, Andrew Green and Gary Snapper

Teaching Caribbean Poetry
Edited by Beverley Bryan and Morag Styles

Teaching Caribbean Poetry

Edited by Beverley Bryan
and Morag Styles

LONDON AND NEW YORK

First published 2014
by Routledge
2 Park Square, Milton Park, Abingdon, Oxon OX14 4RN

and by Routledge
711 Third Avenue, New York, NY 10017

Routledge is an imprint of the Taylor & Francis Group, an informa business

British Library Cataloguing-in-Publication Data
A catalogue record for this book is available from the British Library

Library of Congress Cataloging-in-Publication Data
Teaching Caribbean poetry / edited
   by Beverley Bryan and Morag Styles.
      pages cm
   Includes bibliographical references and index.
   1. Caribbean poetry (English)—Study and teaching.   I. Bryan, Beverley,
1949-   II. Styles, Morag.
   PR9205.A53T44 2013
   810.9'9729071—dc23
   2013014581

ISBN: 978-0-415-64047-3 (hbk)
ISBN: 978-0-415-64048-0 (pbk)
ISBN: 978-0-203-08272-0 (ebk)

Typeset in Galliard
by Apex CoVantage, LLC

MIX
Paper from
responsible sources
FSC   FSC® C013056
www.fsc.org

Printed and bound in Great Britain by
TJ International Ltd, Padstow, Cornwall

Contents

Notes on contributors

Editors

Beverley Bryan is Professor of Language Education at the University of the West Indies' Mona School of Education and a past Head of Department and Director of the School of Education. She has over 20 publications in refereed journals and as chapters in books on cross-cultural issues in Language and Literature Education; vernacular concerns in Creole situations; teacher formation; and literacy curricula and policy. She is the author of two books, including *The Heart of Race* (with Suzanne Scafe and Stella Dadzie). Her latest book is on language teaching in a Creole-speaking environment: *Between Two Grammars: Research and Practice on Language Learning and Teaching in a Creole-speaking Environment*. She is Caribbean Coordinator of the Teaching Caribbean Poetry Project in collaboration with Cambridge University.

Morag Styles is Professor of Children's Poetry at the University of Cambridge's Faculty of Education, and a Fellow of Homerton College. She divides her time between teaching and research. She has organised numerous international conferences, and exhibitions at the Fitzwilliam Museum and the British Library. Publications include *From the Garden to the Street: 300 Years of Poetry for Children, Children Reading Pictures: Interpreting Visual Texts, Reading Lessons From the Eighteenth Century: Mothers, Children and Texts* and *Poetry and Childhood*. She is currently directing a Caribbean Poetry Project in collaboration with the University of the West Indies.

Contributors

Lorna Down is a senior lecturer in Education in the School of Education, University of the West Indies. She has published widely in the areas of Literature and Education for Sustainable Development. She has also co-authored a number of language textbooks. Her current research focus is in the field of Literature Education, Education for Sustainable Development and Teacher Education.

Georgie Horrell is a lecturer and tutor at the University of Cambridge's Faculty of Education. She has taught in both South Africa and the UK—in high schools as well as tertiary institutions. She has a vibrant, wide-ranging interest in post-colonial and children's literatures and has published a number of articles in these fields.

Roz Hudson was a head of English in north London and former head-teacher of Alexandra Park School, which is centrally involved in the Caribbean Poetry Project. She is currently a research associate of the Centre for Commonwealth Education at Cambridge Faculty of Education.

Mervyn Morris is Professor Emeritus of Creative Writing and West Indian Literature at the University of the West Indies, Mona and an internationally acclaimed poet. From 1966 until 2002, he was on the staff of the University of the West Indies, Mona. He is the author of *'Is English We Speaking' and Other Essays* (1999), *Making West Indian Literature* (2005) and *I Been There, Sort Of: New and Selected Poems* (2006).

Sharon Phillip is a lecturer in the Teaching of English at the School of Education, University of the West Indies, St Augustine, Trinidad and Tobago. Her research interests and professional presentations include Caribbean Poetry, Children's Literature, Professional Development, and Critical Thinking. She taught at primary and secondary levels before moving on to tertiary education.

Velma Pollard is a retired senior lecturer in Language Education in the Department of Educational Studies, Faculty of Arts and Education of the University of the West Indies at Mona, Jamaica. Her major research interests have been Creole Languages of the Anglophone Caribbean, the Language of Caribbean Literature and Caribbean Women's Writing. She has published a handbook: *From Jamaican Creole to Standard English: A Handbook for Teachers* (1994, 2003) and a monograph: *Dread Talk: the language of Rastafari* (1994, 2000).Velma Pollard has published poems and stories in regional and international journals and anthologies. She has a novel, three collections of short fiction and five books of poetry on the market. Her novella *Karl* won the Casa de las Americas prize in 1992.

Sandra Robinson is a lecturer in Language Arts Education at the University of the West Indies, Cave Hill Campus, where she also coordinates the undergraduate Bachelors of Education programme. She has special interest in the nature and acquisition of professional knowledge and expertise of teachers of English. Her current research focuses on the learning and development of teachers of English and the interaction between teachers and learners in the English classroom. She coordinates the University of the West Indies, Cave Hill segment of the Caribbean Poetry Project (CPP) workshops for teachers in the Eastern Caribbean.

Aisha Spencer is a lecturer in the Department of Language, Literacy and Literature at the Mico University College in Kingston, Jamaica and a part-time lecturer in the School of Education at the University of the West Indies, Mona Campus. She is also a doctoral candidate in the Department of Literatures in English at the University of the West Indies, Mona. Her primary research interests and journal publications have focused on gender and nation in the Caribbean.

David Whitley is a lecturer in the Faculty of Education at Cambridge University, where he teaches film, poetry and children's literature. He is particularly interested in the way the arts offer different forms of understanding and engagement with the natural world. He has contributed to debates about the teaching and dissemination of poetry in a variety of different contexts, including editing *Poetry and Childhood* (2010) and contributing to the Caribbean Poetry Project. He has published articles on Ted Hughes, William Wordsworth, Chaucer, Carol Ann Duffy and Aesop's fables. His most recent book is an ecocritical study of Disney animation, *The Idea of Nature in Disney Animation: From Snow White to WALL•E* (2012).

Preface

Teachers and students reading literature from a region of which they have no experience will often call for help. *Teaching Caribbean Poetry* belongs with the first responders.

This helpful book discusses a number of poems by Caribbean authors (writing from home or in the diaspora), and offers useful information about cultural contexts and the changing features of what Kamau Brathwaite called 'the tentative cultural norm . . . not whole or hard . . . but cracked, fragmented, ambivalent, not certain of itself, subject to shifting lights and pressures' (Brathwaite, 1974: 6). The brief contributions here—and they identify fuller treatments of anglophone Caribbean poetry—will be of assistance not only to educators from outside the Caribbean, negotiating the particularities of West Indian literature, but also to many West Indians, who often know little about Caribbean territories other than their own.

The product of extensive collaboration, the book shares teaching strategies developed in the West Indies and the United Kingdom and it reports on the responses in varying situations. Resistance to poetry dwindles in the face of well-planned activity in the classroom or creative workshop. Facts not previously known may be bridges to understanding. Maps, photographs, films and material available on the internet, may bring the reader closer to what initially seems foreign. Hearing accents that reflect a poem's regional origin can engage and clarify. The project has made 'the oral, aural and performative aspects of Caribbean poetry— the *sound* of it—as central as the written word' (Introduction, p. 2). *Poetry Archive*, with poets reading their work, is an invaluable resource.

When the teaching has gone well, there should be deeper, subtler, more accurate appreciation of the poems, a closer focus on their language; and recognition, emphasised in the project, that 'Caribbean poetry is not just about the vernacular but involves the full range of linguistic devices available in the region, as well as a startling range of voices' (Introduction, p. 3).

Mervyn Morris

Acknowledgements

Beverley Bryan and Morag Styles would like to thank all the contributors to this book for their hard work and willingness to share their expertise in Caribbean poetry. In addition, special thanks are due to Mervyn Morris, a stalwart of the project from the outset, for reading the manuscript and writing the preface. We are grateful to Roz Hudson for introducing us to the work of Tessa Ware and Crispin Bonham-Carter, teachers at Alexandra Park School, Haringey, London, both of whom are represented in this volume.

In addition, some notable poets have contributed to our project and inspired us to write this book. Special mention must be made of those teaching and performing on our courses in the Caribbean and UK on which the book is based—John Agard, Anthony Joseph, Mark McWatt, Kei Miller, Mervyn Morris, Philip Nanton, Grace Nichols, Esther Phillips and Dorothea Smartt. Working with teachers from many different territories in the Eastern Caribbean would not have been possible without the help of Dr. Didacus Jules, Registrar of CXC, Dr. Jennifer Obidah, Director of the School of Education, Cave Hill, Barbados and the relevant Ministries of Education; it was master-minded by Sandra Robinson, working with her colleague at Cave Hill, Samuel Soyer, and supported by research assistants Karen Thomas and Gina Burnham.

We would like to thank both our universities for enabling us to work on this exciting project—the University of Cambridge Centre for Commonwealth Education at the Faculty of Education and the University of the West Indies at Mona, Cave Hill and St Augustine campuses. We are also grateful to Mike Younger, who made the project possible in the first place and has facilitated it ever since, to Bryony Horsley-Heather, who administers the project and who proofread and presented the final manuscript, and to Sally Roach and Ruth Kühn at the Centre for Commonwealth Education, Cambridge. We are also grateful to members of our advisory panel, including Bea Colley, Ally Smith and Helen Taylor.

Finally, we would like to thank Richard Carrington on behalf of the Poetry Archive and Jeremy Poynting of Peepal Tree Press, both of whom are partners in this project. We are grateful for the generosity of Peepal Tree Press for permission to quote 'Love Overgrows a Rock' by Eric Roach in its entirety.

This book would not have been possible without our sponsors, the Commonwealth Education Trust, and we are particularly grateful to Judy Curry and John Picknett for their unfailing enthusiasm and support.

Introduction

Why Caribbean poetry?

Beverley Bryan and Morag Styles

In writing a book on this subject, we have to consider: why Caribbean poetry? Why has a programme of this scope been put together to promote a particular educational and creative enterprise above all others? There must be some special reason for it and indeed there is. We cannot cover all the features of Caribbean poetry but our book will introduce some of what we see as the defining characteristics of this body of work that we want to make available to more people—especially the young in schools. They will be our ultimate audience and by default, the teachers who must engage them.

Caribbean poetry is a relatively new area of literature, which has developed its specific features over the last hundred years. Perhaps, it is the newness that gives it a certain vibrancy and joy, what Brown and McWatt (2005: xvii) call 'the most life-affirming and spiritually uplifting body of poetry'. They are suggesting that this is poetry that will enrich the spirit as the reader engages.

An ocean apart—a shared vision

This book is the natural outcome of a course on Teaching Caribbean Poetry (TCP), which has been developed by lecturers in English and Education at the University of Cambridge Faculty of Education and the University of the West Indies (UWI). This initiative is part of a bigger Caribbean Poetry Project (CPP) that has been underway since 2010 to promote and enhance the teaching of Caribbean poetry in schools in the Caribbean and the UK. The course itself covers the range of Caribbean poetry we think it is important for students to know about. The 'we' refers to the CPP team consisting of four members from UWI, Jamaica (Mona), one from UWI, Barbados (Cave Hill), one from UWI, Trinidad (St Augustine), and four from the University of Cambridge. In addition, we are working with distinguished poets, Mervyn Morris, Mark McWatt and others as one commitment of the project is to include poets as teachers. So far, the TCP course has been taught as a full programme in Jamaica and Cambridge, UK, and as a series of workshops in Antigua and Barbuda, Barbados, Dominica, St Kitts and Nevis, Grenada, Guyana, London, UK, St Lucia, Montserrat and Anguilla, St Vincent and the Grenadines and Trinidad and Tobago. One of the aims of our project was to increase the exposure of Caribbean poets on the online Poetry Archive (www.poetryarchive.co.uk) and we have made a good start in that direction. There are many references to poets and poems on the Archive in this book.

Although separated by an ocean, one of the joys of this project was discovering how much was shared by like-minded colleagues in the Caribbean and the UK. We quickly found that what united us was our love of poetry, our passion for teaching it, and our shared regret that in both parts of the world poetry struggles to be taught confidently by teachers and enjoyed and understood by pupils. Our joint mission, therefore, was to devise a poetry course that appreciated the difficulties under which teachers are working, the various constraints on the curriculum and the need to find ways to make it accessible to the young without losing its challenge. We put poets working with teachers and pupils at the heart of our project making the oral, aural and performative aspects of Caribbean poetry—the *sound* of it—as central as the written word. Other factors, like exam syllabi in both parts of the world, were taken into account and we also decided that although our concern was Caribbean poetry, this book would offer insights into teaching poetry generally. Finally, appreciating the demands on teachers and knowing how hard it can be to motivate young people, we have tried to provide both the background to the poetry and ways of teaching it successfully. The final chapters of this book are devoted to the latter.

Histories of Caribbean poetry

In considering Caribbean poetry, we are dealing with a body of work that is not just stirring and heartening, dynamic and amusing, musical and linguistically varied—though it is all those things. Some of the poetry is tough because Caribbean poetry deals with powerful and potent content. Most consistent and evocative is the attention it devotes to the politics and history of the region, which covers a troubling yet compelling canvas. In Chapter 4 we consider the roots *and routes* of some of these traumatic events, challenging the familiar Eurocentric perspective. The poetry moves us from the visceral experience of slavery, to colonial government, to independence, and to the post-colonial questioning of what that history means and how it has positioned Caribbean people in a globalised world. Our discussion of the poetry suggests that because of that history, many Caribbean people (including poets, of course) have been drawn to a metropolitan exile in America, Canada, Britain and other places and, for some, they only become truly Caribbean in exile, missing what they have lost. The poetry reflects the unsettling nature of identity for many Caribbean people, some of whom live far away from their roots, and champions the experience of the marginalised, questioning the status quo (see especially Chapters 4 and 6). This is true of poets as varied as Derek Walcott, Kamau Brathwaite, Linton Kwesi Johnson, Louise Bennet and Bob Marley, names that will become familiar to readers of this book. At the same time, Caribbean people seek through the migration experience to 'mek life' in Lorna Goodison's words or, as Grace Nichols puts it, 'To tell you de truth / I don't know really where I belaang' but 'Anywhere I hang me knickers is home' (2010). New generations of poets, such as Kei Miller, are keen to fashion something beautiful *and* authentic from the vicissitudes of history.

Nation language

Apart from the sense of history that pervades Caribbean poetry, another important feature is the presence of the vernacular, the indigenous language spoken in the Caribbean, referred to by Brathwaite as *nation language*. This is the political and cultural term used to describe the Creoles of the region, illustrated by a variety of voices with different accents, registers and dialects. In a slim but seminal text, *History of the Voice,* Brathwaite testifies to the privileging of the voice and the oral tradition by reference to well-known *sound* poets in the region. *Voiceprint* (Brown et al., 1989) was a major departure in poetry anthologies in its attempt to capture the voice in its manifold cadences, reflecting this oral culture that includes songs, stories and prayers from private and public forums—from the preacher to the politician. The unique contribution of dub poetry, with its antecedents in reggae, is also given serious attention (Brown and McWatt, 2005). Our book includes a specific chapter on the language of Caribbean poetry (see Chapter 2). But a word of caution; Caribbean poetry is not just about the vernacular but involves the full range of linguistic devices available in the region, as well as a startling range of voices.

A musical aesthetic

The language of Caribbean poetry is accessible but at the same time quite daring in what it manages to do with form; many poets are technically adventurous, using, for example, jazz-like rupture and subversion of rhythm. The oral culture includes a medley of forms and registers in a heritage of song, speech and performance and so a related cultural phenomenon is the musical aesthetic, explicated by the way rhythm and sound has helped to define the poetry (see especially Chapter 3). The calypso tradition illustrates that well in combining the history of struggle and resistance through mockery—another assertive attempt by enslaved Africans to 'mek life'. Reggae is a later instrument of resistance, which the distinguished poet and scholar Kwame Dawes refers to as 'the aesthetic which has come to shape the creative context for much of the writing that has emerged out of the Caribbean in the last two decades' (1999: 8). For Dawes the music, reggae, is now the vehicle, the dominant path, to understanding the meanings of this 'post-colonial moment' (to rehearse a much used phrase). In making the links to reggae then we also consider Rasta culture and its continuity with the African homeland. The diversity of culture in the Caribbean celebrates hybridity—the mixture of people and practices from many places, regenerated anew. As Brown (2007) notes:

> if anything can be said to define West Indian poetry it is that sense of an engagement with the diverse and often hidden sources of Caribbean history and culture and the determination to refashion those materials into poetry which speaks of and into the present in voices that the peoples of the region would recognise as their own.
>
> (Brown, 2007: 155)

The physical environment

Another critical feature of Caribbean poetry is the awareness of its own space, which we have referred to as a sense of place. Often the poems are rooted in the physical environment, describing the landscapes and seascapes and the writers' connection to them. We explore that arc of meaning from the physical to the psychological, moving from sensuous memories of Caribbean childhoods, noticing and valuing the surrounding natural world, to an inner space 'where our most intimate and intricate connections to the world are grounded' (see Chapter 1, p. 5), thus deepening our conception of the environment. In Chapter 1, we focus on a poem by Eric Roach, 'Love Overgrows a Rock', to understand and articulate Roach's ambivalent relationship with the circle of islands that we call the Caribbean. Later, we examine poets' varying perspectives of the Caribbean, often most poignant and powerful when written about from afar, or on returning home (see for example, 'Reggae fi Dada' in Chapter 6 and 'The Light of the World' in Chapter 5).

Poetry in many voices

A singularly important thread of voices in Caribbean poetry that is reflected in this book is that of women—from early pioneers like Una Marson and Louise Bennett to the medley of fine works by a range of female voices during the twentieth and twenty-first centuries, including that of Olive Senior, taking up the themes that are common in Caribbean poetry, often subtly engendered. More recently, younger female voices such as those of Jennifer Rahim (Trinidad), Tanya Shirley (Jamaica) and Dorothea Smartt (Barbados) have opened up new ways of writing and thinking about the experience of women in the Caribbean.

Inevitably, we have highlighted some of the best known poets of the region, partly because their poetry will be familiar to readers and a good place to start when thinking about teaching Caribbean poetry, partly because their work is so good that we are spoiled for choice of poems and partly because we could not write a book about Caribbean poetry without their presence. Some of these poets are represented in chapters 6 and 7 and a whole chapter is devoted to the work of Derek Walcott (Chapter 5). Even so, we have neglected more poets than we have celebrated and for that we are very sorry. Hard choices had to be made and we regret the impossibility of including all those who deserve attention. One choice we did make was to try to include a good number of poets who live in the Caribbean as well as those who moved on to the USA, Canada and the UK.

It should be noticeable to readers that in this volume we often focus on the poem. This is necessary and instructive of our intention as readers and teachers to encourage students to pay attention to what a poem has to say and how it says it. We have been careful to select poems that are worthy of careful analysis, sometimes less well known to the average teacher in the Caribbean or UK. We hope to have provided models for approaching a wide range of poetry. On the other hand, we have not neglected well loved, foot-tapping poems that amuse, sing, dance and invite a lively response in their readers. We want students to engage with, and become part of, that special experience that poets try to create through the words on the stage and on the page.

The collaboration that has developed over the last few years between our two universities has sought to enhance the knowledge and teaching of Caribbean poetry among secondary/high school students in the UK and West Indies through courses and workshops. This book takes the project one step further in sharing the research and practice of academics and practitioners from both settings who embarked on this journey to share Caribbean poetry with teachers and children. We hope the readers of this book will travel with us and, indeed, move beyond us in appreciating, celebrating and promoting this powerful body of poetry.

Chapter 1

Poetry, place and environment

The scope of Caribbean poetry

David Whitley

Poetry . . . Place . . . Environment—the rich connections between these areas, each understood with powerful historical roots binding them together, constitute much of the underpinning for the Caribbean Poetry project. Of the three, though, 'Environment' is perhaps the most problematic to grasp in its full significance initially. The word seems to suggest something 'out there' that we've become vaguely responsible for; the world conceived as vulnerable, a politicised arena. The word 'environment' implies an objectified space, defined through science. It takes its bearings from the conflict between economic goals and conservation strategies, from the contradictions generated by our fractured understandings of nature.

In running a thread of environmental consciousness through the project, though, we are not just making a special case for its relevance to the extraordinary body of poetry that has grown from a particular region and set of histories in the Caribbean. We want to develop the concept of environment here as signifying an inner space within the heart and mind, as well as a term we use for something apart from us that increasingly urges moral and political responsibilities upon us. Poetry is particularly attuned—centred even—on this inner space, where our most intimate and intricate connections to the world are grounded. Plants and animals are part of the very texture of poetic thought; and poetry, of all the arts, is the most closely connected to the earth. Moreover environment, properly conceived, is not a specialised domain, but encompasses all the processes that are most primary at the very foundations of life. We start, then, with two apparently simple and highly accessible poems that embody something of this perception of poetry's attunement to environment at the centre of life.

Let us consider first James Berry's (2004: 83–4) seemingly artless recollection of the sights, sounds, tastes and smells of his childhood in a Jamaican village. The full poem, 'Childhood Tracks', is available with an evocative reading by James Berry, on the Poetry Archive website.

> Eating crisp fried fish with plain bread
> Eating sheared ice made into 'snowball'
> with syrup in a glass.
> Eating young jelly-coconut mixed
> With village-made wet sugar,
> Drinking cool water from a calabash gourd
> On worked land in the hills.
>
>   . . .
>
> Seeing children toy-making in a yard
> while slants of evening sunlight slowly disappear.
> Seeing an evening's dusky hour lit up
> by dotted lamplight.
> Seeing fishing nets repaired between canoes.

Berry's poem is developed in the most straightforward of forms—the list. Individual memory impressions are gathered together in verse paragraphs that are categorised through the senses: first taste, then smell, hearing, sight. The poet's childhood is thus recollected through images whose sensuous details evoke strong connective feeling for a particular place and way of life. Although some of the images are near universal, and would be recognised as common to many different rural areas of the globe reaching back across history, quite a number are specific to the Caribbean. If this evocation of childhood in relation to the customs of rural, village life shares something with pastoral poetry generally, then, the poem's grounding in particularities of place also gives it a distinctive quality of its own.

The poem in focus

In many ways this is a very straightforward poem and the pleasure of reading it (or hearing it read) comes from the way the images conjure sense impressions with a feeling of immediacy and 'thereness'. These sense impressions are aggregated to create an insider's viewpoint of a particular kind of childhood. The poem takes the reader back to the experience of a particular time and place by re-presenting details that both typify a way of life and hold a special, personal resonance for the speaker. There are a couple of other angles that the poem usefully sets up, though, which may take us a little further in understanding the links between poetry, place and environment that we began exploring above.

First, the poem makes us aware, unobtrusively but insistently, that this is a working environment. The focus throughout is on the food, plants and animals that—at least in the speaker's memory—epitomise ordinary patterns of work and consumption within rural, farming life in mid-twentieth-century Jamaica. Thus, even the simple act of drinking cool water from a calabash gourd takes place in the context of 'worked land on the hills'. Again, the joyful sound of children laughing is heard, not while they play at leisure, but as they collectively perform the useful task of carrying water back to the village. In classical terms, the poem is a kind of 'georgic'.[1] It records the details of rural working life in a natural world that requires steady human effort to supply the necessary essentials of daily life.

The second angle that should perhaps be borne in mind, however, is that the images in the poem express a kind of innocence that is viewed elegiacally, over distance and time. Details of the poet's childhood are recalled vividly, but also, to some extent, nostalgically. (James Berry published this poem in 2004, when he was 80, over half a century after he had left Jamaica to make a new home for himself in England. Does this make a difference to the way we read and respond to the poem?) In a different context, the details that convey a childlike innocence in the poem could easily be seen from harder-edged, more problematic, 'fallen' perspectives. The 'village-made wet sugar', for instance (a delicious additional sweetener for the child's treat of 'young jelly-coconut'), is differentiated from the sugar production that defines so much Caribbean history and identity, with its root deep in slavery. Here sugar is for local use, unrefined, lip-smackingly wet, and innocent of its dark historical antecedents. Similarly with the smells, tastes and colours of other produce of the land. From another—more modern—point of view, these could be seen as 'commodities' produced within an unequal system of exchange for increasingly unstable global markets. In this child-centred poem, though, the produce of the earth is savoured—in all its unalienated materiality—as items displayed for local consumption, 'owned' by the community. Pineapples are smelled 'fermenting' in 'stillness of hot sunlight', rather than being glimpsed in transit to canning factories or packed in refrigerated containers; coffee odours mix in strangely evocative amalgams with 'whiffs' of fish, mango and mint. And banana trees, instead of being corralled into the serried ranks that characterise intensive, agro-industrial monoculture, are seen on a 'tangled land-piece', offering shade to the 'cud-chewing' goats beneath them. The speaker's nostalgic consciousness of his local, 'home' environment is thus conveyed simply and movingly, with apparent purity of tone—but that lyric purity is attained by limiting the point of view to a particular focus.

The poem's relationship to different poetic traditions can also be seen in the way it presents wildlife, and this aspect connects to Valerie Bloom's 'Two Seasons'. Consider the detail of the nightingale, for instance, in the lines—'Hearing a nightingale in song/in moonlight and sea-sound.' This sounds natural enough—and is rather romantic. From the point of view of a European reader, however, the context appears slightly odd. Moonlight is traditionally associated with nightingales (which sing particularly evocatively at night), but the nightingale that comes from Africa to nest in Britain every summer is a shy, woodland bird that would hardly ever be heard near the sea. So the mixing of the bird's song with 'sea-sound' is registered as something of a dislocation, a strange new environment for the bird to be heard within, on a tropical island. Probably no bird is more richly imbricated within the English poetic tradition, too—Chaucer, Spenser, Shakespeare, Keats, Coleridge and Clare (among many others) have all written famous poems featuring the nightingale. Berry would probably have encountered a number of these poems as part of the colonial education he received in Jamaica before the Second World War. He would also have heard birds called nightingales in Jamaica when he was growing up, as he recalls here. But they are not the same bird. There are no Old World nightingales (*Luscinia megarhynchos*) in the Western hemisphere. The name was given to several different species in the Americas and the Caribbean by colonists, in order to forge a nostalgic connection with their homelands. The singling out of this detail is thus more complex than might at first appear. One could see it as a kind of affiliation to a rich tradition within English poetry, but as also marked by difference, a re-appropriation in another geographical and cultural context.

This marking of difference while asserting equivalence is also displayed, in a much more overt and sustained form, in Valerie Bloom's 'Two Seasons' (2000). This poem is also available in its entirety, with an excellent reading by the poet, on the Poetry Archive. A sense of place, established here through comparison with more northern countries, is one of the most important angles to be taken up within Caribbean poetry. Bloom's poem provides a very useful introduction to many of the underlying issues involved in shaping identity along such a comparative axis. The poem affiliates the reader firmly to a Caribbean context, but the comparison with climatic features of more northern countries that is used to frame each stanza suggests that the author (if not the speaker of the poem) occupies an evaluative position in between different cultures and places. Although she is of a younger generation than Berry, Bloom shares his experience of emigration, having settled in England in 1979, when she was in her early twenties.

> We don' have a Springtime like some folk
> Who live in dem colder place,
> but we have a time when de soft rain come,
> an' tease open de seedcase
> o' de poincianna and de trumpet tree,
> An whisper to de young cane to wake
> when de guangu blossom is pink an' white
> powder-puff, prettying up de earth face.
> But not Spring like in dem colder place.

The poem in focus

Bloom's poem appears straightforward and accessible: like Berry's, it engages the reader through evoking the sensuous detail of selective features in the speaker's natural environment. The tone and point of view through which these details are presented are slightly more complex than may at first appear, however. The syntax would seem to suggest that the details selected to characterise the Caribbean climate and environment are being offered to mitigate an innate sense of lack or deficit. 'We don' have . . . We don' have . . . We don' have', Bloom intones at the start of each stanza, with a soft, plangent inflection that might be construed as carrying with it just a hint of gentle regret, or even apology. Anyone who accepts this interpretation of the refrain as a premise for understanding the whole poem, however, will soon find themselves being re-educated. For, if the poem is an 'apology', then this needs to be understood as consonant with the older usage of the word, as in Sir Philip Sidney's *Apologie for Poetrie*. This was really an assertion of inherent value, an ardent defence of poetry. Bloom's poem might be better perceived, in this sense, as didactic. It begins by seeming to offer a stance within which the Caribbean is seen as inherently deficient by comparison with northern countries (it only has two seasons rather than four—less variety, less contrast, by implication). And then it turns this around by allowing details of the Caribbean environment to assert either equivalence or greater intensity. Thus the lack of a European autumn or American fall is countered by the vividness with which the flame tree lights up the forest 'like a fireball'. This is offered with sublime colour contrasts, as in 'de blue mahoe leaf dem turn bright bronze', that would surely rival even the most glorious fall in New England.

In celebrating the variety of sensuous experience offered in the Caribbean environment through the sequence of the year, the poem conjures images of distinctive kinds of flora and fauna that are mainly identified by their local names. Thus, although the general reader will easily recognise generic classes such as tree frog, almond, grasshopper and bee, they will also encounter a particular species of grackle (*Holoquiscalus lugubris luminosus*), which looks a little like the European blackbird and is given its Jamaican name, 'cling-cling', and the 'peeni-wallie', a local name for the moth-like lantern, or candle fly. A number of trees and plants—poinciana, mahoe, guangu,[2] fee-fee—also appear with their indigenous titles, though without causing any substantial difficulty for non-native readers, since the distinctive colours of their blossoms or foliage are vividly described. The names, together with the idiomatic use of Jamaican Creole more generally, nevertheless have the effect of centring the poem within a strongly localised consciousness, an effect that is reinforced by the speaker's adopting the plural pronoun 'we', affiliating herself to a distinctively West Indian group identity. In a sense the poem is both teaching young readers from outside about the Caribbean, as well as instilling a sense of pride and recognition in those who live there.

The richness of local names and species in Bloom's poem is significant in another way, too, since the poem could be seen as a reworking of a well-known poem from the colonial era that many Jamaican children still learn by heart in school. This source poem is H.D. Carberry's 'Nature' (1995), a full text of which is readily available on the internet. Carberry's poem is written in standard English and begins:

> We have neither Summer nor Winter
> Neither Autumn nor Spring.
> We have instead the days
> When the gold sun shines on the lush green canefields –
> Magnificently.

It has a similar didactic strategy to Bloom's, in that it asserts the equivalence (or even enhanced beauty) of what the Jamaican climate and landscape can offer 'instead' of the more northerly countries' seasons. But Bloom's use of Jamaican Creole, combined with much greater abundance of reference to specifically indigenous species, provide the poem with a far stronger centre within a distinctively Caribbean environment. Comparison between the two poems can reveal much about how a tradition has been reworked to speak to a more post-colonial sensibility.

Perhaps the most significant aspect of the features the speaker observes in the Caribbean environment, though, is that they are subject to change. This may seem obvious, especially in a poem that evaluates experience of a climate where there are only two major seasonal variations in the year. But response to change, whether small or large, human-made or natural, is at the centre of environmental consciousness. One of Bloom's strategies in this poem is actually to break up the larger categories of seasonal change, to distinguish the ebb and flow of smaller phenomena within them. There are all kinds of time and transitions in the poem, including the wonderful 'season when mango is king', which, though not officially a 'season', is actually a very distinctive period when the abundance of mangoes in all parts of the island is relished by children especially. The poem also expresses confidence in the earth's ability to restore itself after periods of tumultuous or violent change, such as the hurricane enacts—'the earth always revive, by and by', the poem concludes, with quiet faith in the ordinary processes of renewal.

Teaching the poems

Both these poems are about noticing and valuing things in the world around you. Both demonstrate how poetry can be an especially finely tuned instrument for doing this; it captures everyday sights and sounds, gathering them up in patterns that enable us to think and feel about them afresh. The distinctively Caribbean context also grounds the reader in a strong sense of place, a theme we will examine in wider ranging, more problematic ways when we consider the last poem in this chapter. The primary aim of teaching these poems, then, is to encourage personal kinds of thinking about the ways the senses connect you to environment and place. Below are three suggestions as to how this might be initiated (these are just illustrative examples of course; there are many other ways of working productively with the material and ideas can readily be adapted to the specific needs of classes).

1 To develop connections between poetry and the local, natural environment, ask students to make a list of things they notice and that appeal to them in their own environment. Encourage them to identify a range of things that they experience through different senses, and to include both phenomena in nature and human activities. Get them talking with each other about what makes the things they have singled out memorable for them particularly, and perhaps explore one or two instances of this with the class. Students can then either use their lists as material to shape into a poem of their own, or reflect on how what is noticed by the two poets compares with their own experience.

2 Using the resources of the cyber-environment to develop such connections further, ask students to find pictures on the internet (or elsewhere) of plants, animals, farm produce mentioned in the poems. Share these images with the class, at the same time asking students to relate what they have found out about the items they have researched in this way. (This may uncover patterns of change too—in use of the land, farming, species that have become rarer or more abundant etc.) Return to the poems being read out and ask if students have a different response to them after sharing their images and research.

3   Ask students to consider similarities and differences between Carberry's poem and Bloom's. Carberry's poem uses images of the canefields (first 'lush green', later 'reaped') as a point of anchorage in depicting changes equivalent to 'seasons'. The language evoking the canefields sounds conventionally pastoral. Students may note a parallel innocence of the grim history associated with cane production here to that of Berry's poem. But does the language and context make this 'innocence' more sanitised and deliberately evasive in Carberry? Likewise there are no animals, apart from bees, in the Carberry poem, and there is less sensuous contact and movement than in Bloom. Do students experience the Carberry poem as more 'picturesque'—airbrushed to fit conventional expectations—and static, perhaps?

In the next section, we will examine some of the issues already raised in a wider context. We use a slightly more difficult poem, Eric Roach's 'Love Overgrows a Rock' to develop our initial thoughts further.[3] Here is the text of the poem:

'Love Overgrows a Rock'

Only the foreground's green;
Waves break the middle distance,
And to horizon the Atlantic's spread
Bright, blue and empty as the sky;
My eyot jails the heart,
And every dream is drowned in the shore water.

Too narrow room pressed down
My years to stunted scrub,
Blunted my sister's beauty
And my friend's grave force,
Our tribe's renewing faith and pride:
Love overgrows a rock as blood outbreeds it.

We take banana boats
Tourist, stowaway,
Our luck in hand, calypsos in the heart:
We turn Columbus' blunder back
From sun to snow, to bitter cities;
We explore the hostile and exploding zones.

The drunken hawk's blood of
The poet streams through the climates of the mind
Seeking a word's integrity
A human truth. So from my private hillock
In Atlantic I join cry:
Come, seine the archipelago;
Disdain the sea; gather the islands' hills
Into the blue horizons of our love.

'Love Overgrows a Rock', first published in 1957 and reissued in the Peepal Tree Press edition of Roach's *Collected Poems* in 1992, provides an excellent introduction to a course on Caribbean poetry. Within its brief span it encompasses many of the most important themes and concerns taken up by Caribbean poetry at large. But it also imbues these themes with unusual force—urging the reader to engage with them from different angles and in challenging new forms. It opens up to a whole emotional, physical and even political landscape of the Caribbean in a way that can detonate a series of little time bombs inside the reader's head and heart. It's a little poem that resonates at a number of profound levels and it's a great opener for beginning a journey into the richly pleasurable—but also emotionally tough—territory that this extraordinary literature offers.

The poem in focus

What are the paths that this poem opens into the wider domain of Caribbean poetry then? The first, and perhaps the most significant of these, is the way the poem grounds itself on an unusually austere vision of the land and sea. The poet makes us keenly aware that the home ground from which he speaks is a small island, surrounded by ocean, and linked by affinity to an archipelago of other islands that are stretched out across the Caribbean between the Americas. This may seem like a perfectly ordinary geographical recognition, but it is literally fundamental: for the trenchant particularity of the poet's vision is founded on it. Roach rejects the line of exploration that many other writers take up from this starting point—the tropical profusion, vibrant colour and vitality that this seemingly paradisiacal necklace of islands presents to even the most casual of observers. Instead, he makes the reader keenly aware from the start of limitation. 'Only the foreground's green', he begins descriptively and seemingly innocuously enough. But that 'Only' is a kind of hidden depth charge—as significant in its own way as T.S. Eliot's radical inversion of European perceptions of the vitality of spring in his opening line of 'The Waste Land': 'April is the cruellest month' (1969). Roach deliberately turns away from the life force of the green space, limiting its reach, in a painterly way, to a thin strip in the foreground. Instead his vision turns outwards from the island towards the Atlantic, stretching far out to the horizon, and characterised (although 'Bright, blue') as 'empty as the sky'. The merged horizons of sea and sky seem to lock the speaker into an emotional prison—'My eyot jails the heart'—('Eyot' is a little island). Every aspiration seems to be choked off in this environment ('drowned in the shore water').

It is perhaps worth noting here that the speaker is now oriented towards Africa and Europe, unseen beyond the horizon but situated on the other side of an Atlantic that now defines the scope of the poet's vision. Perhaps there is even a hint—a kind of submerged history—in the waves that break the 'middle distance' of the infamous Middle Passage here. Again though, where other Caribbean poets have reached out imaginatively to Africa as a source of renewal, reaffirming roots, and to Europe to recover an authentic cultural legacy through contestation, Roach limits his vision to the horizon. He is silent about the possibilities of imaginative reconnection. He thus sets his speaker off in a landscape whose confines—the 'narrow room' that defines his expectations in the second stanza—are perceived with stringent and unconsoling clarity. This is the truth of where I am, he seems to be saying.

The second stanza extends these unfulfilled personal emotions to others, suggesting that this is characteristic of a general condition on the island. The youthful beauty of the poet's sister has been 'blunted' by the conditions within which she lives, as has the 'grave force' of his friend. More widely, even the possibility of revitalising cultural and political energies across the region—the 'tribe's renewing faith and pride'—appears thwarted. Written from the perspective of Roach's home island of Tobago in 1957, when political processes in the region were beginning to move gradually towards independence from colonial rule, this is perhaps a surprisingly bleak vision that offers few resources for hope.

There are other potentialities here too, but the stringency of the poem's opening sets up emotional and perceptual challenges for readers, who may be used to seeing the landscape of the Caribbean in rather different ways. Roach's poem is not static though: it has its own line of development and it opens up different pathways in the process of responding to the bleakness of its initial vision of impoverishment and closed down potentialities. The third stanza articulates one significant kind of response: leave the island, try to make a new life in one of the populous cities of the north in Britain or America. Many Caribbean people took this route out in the years after the Second World War. Roach's poem characterises this experience in distinctive ways however. The emotional resilience and optimism of the travellers ('calypsos in the heart') are confronted with coldness, hostility and violence as they come to dwell in the 'exploding zones', the poorer areas within cities defined by conflict. A powerful set of oppositions are activated here ('sun to snow' etc.) in articulating the archetypal experience of diaspora. In some ways the third stanza appears to be as locked in to a process of negation as the first two stanzas, indeed it may seem to consolidate the sense that there is no real way out.

But there is movement here—and energy in the movement—and perhaps that marks a crucial difference? Note too how the poem engages with another archetypal and defining journey, that of Christopher Columbus who, in trying to find a new route through to the spice rich islands of the East Indies, discovered for Europe, instead, the West Indies and Americas. Roach refers to Columbus' journey not as a heroic venture but as a 'blunder', appropriately perhaps, as what Columbus discovered was not at all what he intended, and the colonial histories that his voyage opened up were characterised by the most extreme brutality. But what is most striking here is the way Roach has re-appropriated the image of Columbus' voyage and turned it around, so that it stands as a counterpoint for the West Indians' attempt to find a new life for themselves in the north; and in doing so he makes the meaning of the word 'blunder' twist in potentially new directions. In what sense should we understand the line 'We turn Columbus' blunder back' then? Is the 'turning back' simply a geographical correspondence—Europe to the West Indies: the West Indies to Europe and America? Or is the meaning of 'blunder' changed in the process too, turned back on itself to generate new potentialities? Can a voyage that led ultimately to subjugation for millions of people, in other words, be turned back into a journey towards reclaiming a different kind of future and agency? In the third stanza the negative meanings of blunder seem to apply as much to the West Indian exiles (whom 'we' in the poem are positioned alongside) as to Columbus. But there are buried ambiguities here that the poem will go on to clarify and bring home (literally as well as metaphorically) to readers.

This is the work of the last stanza. Here the energies that are thwarted in the earlier parts of the poem are gathered up again and given a visionary cast that is both inspiring and regenerative. This indeed is the poet's task: to have the courage and determination to uncover a 'human truth'—harsh though this may be—through his commitment to 'word's integrity'; and then to urge reconnection, through the primal instinct of love, with the land and its fellow inhabitants. This is where the ambiguities inherent in the poem's title become alive to the fullest resources of their meaning. The 'Love' that 'overgrows a rock' could be understood as reaching down into every space and hidden fissure in the island, like vegetation growing in tropical profusion. Or, as appears to be the dominant meaning in the first two stanzas, 'overgrows' could be read as effectively 'outgrows', the island not allowing the space for a passionate sense of connection to be adequately realised. The final stanza allows the first meaning to take control, without ever cancelling out the more constricting alternative. The crucial image in the last stanza resides in the poet's exhortation to 'seine the archipelago', since here we are invited to 'join cry' rather than simply to identify with the suffering inherent in a trapped, isolated vision. The metaphor of seine fishing, where the catch is gathered up by drawing in the bottom edge of shallow encircling nets, has a local resonance, since it is widely practised in the Caribbean region. But it is also an image of harvesting natural resources that draws the inhabitants of the whole area—'the archipelago'—together. The poet's vision has turned from the isolated estrangement of his view of the Atlantic (from which we are now urged to free ourselves through 'disdain') and instead moves inwards towards collective affinity with the circling islands of the Caribbean itself. This is home, the poem seems to be saying at the end, simply but profoundly, and we share more in this region of disparate 'eyots', or small islands, than differentiates us.

Teaching the poem

It is clear from this reading of Roach's poem how wide ranging are the implications of its imagery. Its key concerns are also central preoccupations within Caribbean poetry as a whole. How can the poem be best presented then, in a teaching context, so that students can grasp its significance and see it as a bridge, enabling them to begin to engage with key issues within Caribbean poetry more generally in exciting new ways? Three dimensions of the poem are crucial to get in focus, and we'll take each of these in order now.

A sense of place

This poem can convey the feelings engendered by the smallness of many of the Caribbean islands strikingly and thought provokingly. To make this context more concrete and vivid for readers before starting detailed work on the poem, we have found it useful to do some work relating to the literal, geographical space of the Caribbean. Tobago, where Roach lived most of his life, is a hilly, largely volcanic island about 26 miles long by 6 miles wide. Some photographs might be useful to make this literal context more present in the mind for readers, who don't know the area. The strategy we have found most successful though, and that should focus discussion and consciousness for students from all situations, is to show a sequence of maps, starting with the island of Tobago itself and then moving outwards to include the whole of the West Indies, seen in relation to the oceans that surround it and the land mass of the Americas on its outer edges. These images are readily available on the internet. The point needs to be emphasised that it is impossible not to be aware of the sea's surrounding proximity at any place on the island. If you take the map out far enough it is also possible to visualise the vast emptiness of the Atlantic aspect from Tobago, compared to the scattered clustering of islands that constitute the archipelago of the West Indies on the Caribbean side. We have found it productive to ask readers how they might feel about living in this geographical position. The distance between islands, the stretches of ocean that separate them but also the chain through which they appear connected also become clear if represented in this way. A brief discussion of what may characterise 'island mentality' might be useful at this point (perhaps bringing in comparison with Andrea Levy's unravelling of different layers of meaning of 'smallness' in Britain and Jamaica in the post war years, in her recent novel *Small Island*).

Once this work has been done, it becomes much easier for students to engage with the themes in the poem. It may be worth recognising too that Eric Roach chose to remain living and working on his home island of Tobago, despite being tempted to move away, like many other gifted writers of his generation, to lucrative university jobs in the USA and Britain.

This commitment eventually exerted a heavy toll upon him; disillusioned by poverty and a sense of failure he ended up taking his own life in 1974, swimming out to sea from the same bay in neighbouring Trinidad where Columbus was purported to have first landed. Perhaps the movement of the poem towards a reaffirmation and centring of the poet's identity on the hills of his island home become even more moving and poignant in this context though.

In our session we also noted in passing that other Caribbean poets express very different attitudes towards the sea than the sense of an empty, isolating, hostile and at times almost overwhelming horizon that Roach develops in this poem. In Derek Walcott's poetry, for instance, the sea's constant movement represents a kind of freedom. Some teachers might wish to develop comparisons and links with other poetry further in relation to this distinctive theme.

Connections to history

This is one of the most challenging, but also rewarding, areas to engage with when studying Caribbean poetry. Any approach focusing on connections between poetry and history needs to adapt itself to the specific demands made by individual poems, as well as to the knowledge base of the group being taught; so the following notes and suggestions should be used flexibly and adapted to suit particular contexts. One of the challenges faced in teaching 'Love Overgrows a Rock' in an opening session is that, although the poem yields more powerful and penetrating insights if it is understood fully in relation to the histories that shape its tone and meaning, very little of this history is made explicit in the poem itself. The teacher is thus left with a set of decisions to make about teaching strategy: how much of the surrounding history should be made explicit to students and in what form? Whereas it has proved useful to foreground aspects of the sense of place that the poem explores before engaging on work with the poem, we suggest that it may be more productive to approach its connections to history through issues raised by the language of the poem itself. Too much historical information in advance is likely to be experienced as distancing, rather than quickening curiosity and interest.

There are two major points in the poem where focusing discussion on connections to historical processes may be useful, or even decisive, in enabling students to understand and respond fully. The first of these is in relation to the line in the second stanza about 'Our tribe's renewing faith and pride'. A fruitful area for discussion here will focus on Roach's use of the word 'tribe', particularly in the singular, to articulate an emerging cultural and political project. The word obviously associates most strongly with African roots—and students can usefully be asked to assess the significance of this. But it also seems to be used 'poetically' to imply unity, a shared sense of affiliation and identity, not linked to residual elements of any particular tribal culture. With some groups, depending on the degree to which their historical understanding and imaginations are already well developed in this area, it may also be useful to consider the historical provenance of the poem during the period of transition towards independence. What attitudes towards this process are being expressed here? Why might 'faith and pride' be conceived as potentially 'renewing' and why does the poet seem to feel that this process is stunted? This is likely to be touched on only in a light way however, unless the group already have a substantial grounding in Caribbean history of the independence period.

The second point at which history intersects decisively with the poem's direction and meaning is through the comparison of Columbus' voyage with the emigration of contemporary

West Indians from the island. Here the following questions can quicken students' conscious-ness of what is going on in the poem in subtle, open but also potentially compelling forms:

> Why is Columbus' voyage described as a 'blunder'?
> Do you think the islanders' emigration to the northern cities should also be seen as a 'blunder'—or does turning Columbus' blunder back mean changing its meaning?

There is scope for lively and open debate here—on the second question especially—and teachers should be judicious in feeding useful perspectives into the debate to enable it to be as well informed as possible. Sometimes energy and engagement may be more significant than 'facts', which can be sought afterwards if they are felt to be important.

Language

Roach uses Standard English in a relatively formal register in this poem (it is perhaps worth drawing attention to this as it represents a contrastive stance to debates about 'nation lan-guage' that may be introduced later). There are no dialect words in the poem, although words like 'calypso' and 'seine' might be seen as having a Caribbean provenance. The syntax is also not distinctively Caribbean, though there may be a hint of orality in the dropping of the definite article before 'horizon' ('And to horizon the Atlantic's spread'; also in 'Too narrow room . . . '). Nevertheless the language of the poem is striking and crucial in determining how meaning is experienced. The following are suggestions as to how students may be encouraged to become conscious of the language and its effects as they engage with the poem.

The word 'eyot', meaning islet, or little island, in the fifth line is both striking and distinc-tive. Eyot is an Old English word, now so rarely used it will be unfamiliar to most English speakers. It is pronounced 'ate' and the line in which it occurs, 'My eyot jails the heart', is one of the most powerful in the poem. Suggestion—explain what 'eyot' means and how it should be pronounced. Then get students to say the line over to themselves until they are happy they have got the most satisfying intonation for it. Share saying it out loud, then, to others. Ask them how they felt their mouth and face moved when saying the line. Most are likely to register a degree of strain or uncomfortableness—the combination of vowels and consonants in 'My eyot jails . . . ' tends to stretch the mouth back into something between a smile and a grimace if you say the words slowly and carefully. Having acknowledged the physical feeling (and individual variants) discussion may lead on to considering why Roach chose to use such an unusual word for his island home in this line. Note that it is still intimate and possessive, though: 'My eyot . . . '.

Get students to discuss the title of the poem (and the variants of this in the poem itself). Are there different ways we can understand its meaning?

The poem uses alliteration discriminatingly at key points throughout. Ask students to identify one or two points where this happens. Is the alliteration effective in giving a particu-lar charge to the meaning at the points selected?

One of the most interesting and striking phrases towards the end of the poem is 'seine the archipelago'. Having established the meaning of the words and unpacked some of the impli-cations of the metaphor with students, ask them to decide in pairs how the phrase should be spoken. Most people find the phrase deeply pleasurable (perhaps in contrast to the 'eyot' line) to turn around in the mouth. Saying it out loud helps it hang on in the memory and remain available for thought: you also need to decide how dramatically it should be read. It's rather oratorical and grand, but should this aspect be played down or up to mesh with the themes and perspectives of the rest of the poem best?

Finally, the poem develops its meanings rather like a loose limbed sonnet. Each stanza takes up a slightly different perspective or stance, just as the divisions into quatrain, octave, sestet and so on tend to do in the traditional sonnet. Ask students to consider how the emotional tone changes as we move through the stanzas.

It's not necessary to follow all of these suggestions. Just select what seems most likely to advance the dual goals of getting to the heart of the poem and beginning to open up channels that can feed into pleasurable engagement and understanding of Caribbean poetry.

Notes

1 'Georgic' is a variant of pastoral that focuses particularly on farming activities, and sees the land primarily as a working environment.
2 Normally written as guango.
3 We are very grateful to Jeremy Poynting of Peepal Tree Press for generously waiving a fee and giving permission to quote Eric Roach's poem 'Love Overgrows a Rock' in its entirety.

Chapter 2

The language of Caribbean poetry

Aisha Spencer

The 'roots' of Caribbean language in Caribbean poetry

As with any other poetry, the use of language in Caribbean poetry is significant and needs to be looked at carefully in order to understand its meaning. Although the emergence of Caribbean poetry demonstrated colonial influence on the shaping of language and thought in the Caribbean, it was also quite evident that during the post-1940s, a new distinctive form of poetry was developing within (and at times outside of) the Caribbean region. This form had a number of variations and changed over time as it moved from representing 'local experience in traditional [British] forms' (Breiner, 1998: 115) to poetry that '[adjusted] the tradition to [the West Indian] experience' (121) and eventually to the production of a fully transformed type of West Indian poetry that was 'highly politicized' (140). At last Caribbean poets were free to experiment with language in order to represent beliefs, cultural systems and characters reflecting the landscape and life of the Caribbean territories.

In *Twentieth Century Caribbean Literature* (2006), Alison Donnell argues that the traditional English poetic models and constructs that had for centuries shaped and dictated poetic form and content had become inadequate for Caribbean poets during the 1940s and could no longer be seen as the sole models. Some of the poetry by West Indian writers such as Claude McKay, Una Marson, Frank Collymore and the Honourable Louise Bennett-Coverley (from now on called simply Louise Bennett), offered impressions and images of the Caribbean and its cultures, lifestyles and people. The inadequacy of the British literary tradition for these and other Caribbean poets that would later emerge on the literary scene, prompted a new tradition offering alternative views and producing 'a new kind of poetry in English [which] had to be devised to express the realities of language, nature and human experience in a new field of reference governed by new rules of decorum [and] by new values' (Breiner, 1998: 120). Indeed, West Indian poetry began to '[assert] itself against "Europe"' (134).

The nurturing of a distinct Caribbean poetic tradition by Caribbean writers was in many ways dependent on the concept of difference, marked by socio-political realities, history, cultural practices and spiritual beliefs to construct poetry from 'alternative resources' that were largely connected to Africa, rather than Europe. According to Breiner, '[e]ven writers who knew nothing about Africa were excited by the notion that they had an alternative to the European heritage—a tradition equally venerable and complex, but entirely different. The result [was] a revolution in poetry' (Breiner, 1998: 143) and part of that revolution was in the use of language.

Mervyn Alleyne argues that '[the] diversity of linguistic phenomena and language patterns [in Caribbean poetry] is the direct result of the modern post-Columbian history of the region, which witnessed migrations of peoples and population replacements of a scale and complexity perhaps unsurpassed in any other period of equivalent duration in human history' (1985: 3, 4). The languages of these migrants came into sometimes brutal contact with the languages of the colonizers—the Spaniards, the English, the Dutch and the French. The Europeans tried to suppress the various African languages that were brought into the Caribbean territories through the iniquitous slave trade, and so the Creole languages (a mixture of ancestral languages and the languages of the colonizers), were considered inferior. In addition, they were believed to be 'bizarre, aberrant, and corrupt derivatives of one or another European language [and] were not viewed as natural languages with their own rules of grammar' (Alleyne, 1985: 6). This view was held not only by the colonizers but also by many of the Caribbean populations who used these languages. According to Alleyne, what has occurred as a result of these events and perceptions is 'a prejudice against local languages' throughout the Caribbean region (ibid.).

As time went on and emancipation finally brought the promise of freedom to the slaves, the colonial educational systems and policies began to insist on the acquisition of English language by the former slaves. This language policy introduced by the colonizers helped to secure the ideological position that saw English as the superior language. According to Shirley C. Gordon in *A Century of West Indian Education*, there was the need to 'diffuse a grammatical knowledge of the English language as the most important agent of civilization for the coloured population of the colonies' (1963: 58). More than a century later, the imposition of this language policy on newly independent Caribbean territories clearly helped to re-establish notions of the English language having status and power. By the time independence was gained by individual Caribbean territories, English was established as the language of officialdom, of wealth and of high social status. In this context, Creole languages were seen as being bastardized versions of English, inferior and linked to those who lacked intellect and worth. Unfortunately, these perceptions are still held by some in Caribbean societies, even today.

At present, with the exception of a few Caribbean territories, Standard English still holds the label of 'the superior language', while the use of Creole languages tend to be seen as 'suitable for the expression of "folklore" (folktales, folk music, proverbs, etc.) . . .' of Caribbean people (Alleyne, 1985: 6). In most cases, the European language—the formal language—is still considered to be the first language of the people and the Creole languages—the popular and true first languages of the people—are considered inferior, though much linguistic research demonstrates the lexical, phonological and grammatical integrity of them.

The language continuum in the Caribbean ranges from the use of what linguists have termed the 'basilect' or the 'purest' form (Alleyne, 1985) of Creole language to the 'acrolect' or near Standard English. Between these poles there is a series of middle forms labelled the 'mesolect'. It is important to note, however, that Creole languages are usually lexically related to the official language, and that a word may carry one meaning in the official language and a different meaning in the Creole. In Jamaican Creole, for example, the word 'ignorant' refers to an individual behaving in an angry manner while in Standard English it refers to someone lacking knowledge. Another example can be found in *From Jamaican Creole to Standard English: A Handbook for Jamaican Teachers* (1993), by Velma Pollard, where she illustrates how the word 'favour' to the Creole speaker means 'to resemble' while for the Standard English speaker it means 'to be preferred' (Pollard, 1993: 2).

In addition to what has been outlined about the language situation in the Caribbean, there is too the concept of 'nation language', which was formally presented by Kamau Brathwaite in a lecture given to students at Harvard University in 1979, later published by New Beacon

Books: *History of the Voice: The Development of Nation Language in Anglophone Caribbean Poetry* (1984). In this book, Brathwaite clearly establishes his belief in the alternative language of the Caribbean people through the concept coined 'nation language'. Nation language is 'the kind of English spoken by the people who were brought to the Caribbean, not the official English now, but the language of slaves and labourers, the servants who were brought in by the conquistadors' (5–6). Nation language referred then to a new way of using language, that allowed for possibilities of meaning that are not achievable through the 'imperial' uses of the English or any other language, 'imposed' on the Caribbean by the colonizers but instead are 'influenced very strongly by the African model, the African aspect of our New World/ Caribbean heritage' (13). It takes varying forms based on the existing Creoles from across the different Caribbean regions, and the different structures and code-strategies of Creole in one distinct region. It also is identified with distinct rhythms and sounds, which enable the employment of 'not only semantic but *sound* elements' (Brathwaite, 1984: 33), often evoked through the way words are made to function within the poem. Later, in the genre of dub poetry, Rastafarian language was often linked with the dominant use of the drums and, of course, the beat associated with Reggae music.

Nation language, for Brathwaite, should not be labelled as 'dialect' as '[that] carries with it very pejorative overtones' (13). (For the purposes of this chapter too, we will avoid using the term 'dialect', though this is the word often used by Louise Bennett in her discussions of the language she employed in her poetry.) There are a number of features of nation language that will help readers to identify its use in Caribbean poetry: the use of vocabulary and images that originate from or are deeply associated with the Caribbean; the presence of Caribbean folklore in its poetic representation; the presence of community and the representation of the plight of the masses in some way; its use of a plurality of languages; the dominance of the oral tradition; and the distinctly Caribbean sound of the rhythm it produces. Nation language is explained by Brathwaite as operating within historical and poetic representations of the Caribbean experience. He celebrates the concept of difference where it concerns 'the process of using English in a different way from the 'norm'' (1984: 5), and feels it is necessary that we value the strong influence of Africa on the lexical features, uses and sounds of nation language that have been so artfully sewn into the fabric of the poetry coming out of the Caribbean.

There is some controversy over the term 'nation language' however and not all Caribbean poets and scholars agree with all Brathwaite's precepts. For the purposes of this chapter, nation language will represent the distinctive language of Caribbean people as is specifically reflected in the poetic works of particular Caribbean writers. It is important however, as Brathwaite himself asserts, that we do not come to any Caribbean poem with an expectation of how nation language must be framed. What we have to do as readers is to accept the way Caribbean language has been used by the poet, and consider the reasons for his or her particular use of language. To choose to use nation language rather than Standard English is to demonstrate a rejection of the British literary tradition as superior and to resist concepts or ideas tied to European values and beliefs. There are times, however, when the more general term 'Caribbean language' will be used.

Exploring the uses of Caribbean language in Caribbean poetry

In trying to understand and interpret Caribbean poetry, readers have to know that there is not always a set of rules to follow. There are however, as outlined at the start of this chapter, various concepts that can aid in the reader's efforts to meaningfully engage with poems that fall within this category. The aim at this point therefore is to select particular Caribbean poems and examine the way Caribbean language functions in these cases. We are not able to offer a 'tidy' formula with which to approach language in Caribbean poetry, but we hope to raise some useful pointers along the way.

Before the twentieth century, poetry from the West Indies had embedded within it models and forms of British origin, such as the pastoral, epics, odes, heroic couplets and the use of blank verse. In addition, there would have been the dominant presence of British English, which would have been flawlessly represented by Caribbean writers in their efforts to demonstrate that they were able to create literary works that could be placed in the same elevated spaces as the Western literature they had studied. Between the 1920s and the 1950s, however, poets such as Marson, McKay and Collymore also attempted to reflect the notion of 'difference' in their poems, by making reference to Caribbean uses of language. This can be seen in poems such as Marson's 'Kinky Hair Blues' where she uses a form of Creole that is mixed with the African-American language that Delia Jarrett-Macauley (1998: 84) states, 'stirred' Marson deeply, influencing her style while representing a Caribbean-like voice and experience. In 'Kinky Hair Blues', the persona comments on the alienated experience she is subjected to because of the kind of hair she possesses: she 'gwine find a beauty shop cause [she] ain't a lovely belle'. Both traces of the Caribbean and African-American modes of expression can be heard through 'gwine' and 'ain't' respectively. She compares the texture of her hair to the texture of those 'oder young gals/so slick and smart', again fusing together the intonation of the Caribbean/African-American, highlighting the fact that she is writing on behalf of the black race, rather than the beliefs and cultures emanating from Eurocentric systems.

McKay's 'Two-An-Six', written even earlier in 1912, highlights a similar attempt to include a distinct Caribbean tone through the presentation of the common market day experience, which captures both the traditional practice of the Caribbean people and the language of the common folk that would be a significant part of the market day environment.

> Merry voices chatterin'
> Nimble feet dem patterin'
> Big an' little, faces gay,
> Happy day dis market day.
>
> Sateday, de marnin' break,
> Soon soon market people wake . . .
>   (1992, http://www.poemhunter.com/poem/two-an-six/)

The poem opens with the Creole voice describing the locale as being dominated by 'merry voices chatterin' and 'nimble feet dem patterin' and describing the 'hard-wuk'd donkey on the road/trotting wid him ushal load'. Throughout the poem, McKay consistently uses the Creole voice to represent the poverty and hardships faced by the masses who both buy and sell in this market. 'Cousin Sun is lookin' sad/as de market is so bad / . . . '. Having had to sell his sugar for much less than he had bargained for, he feels defeated and frustrated. Yet when he arrives home, his wife raises his spirits, encouraging him to give thanks that they are able to pay for expenses, even if there is no surplus with which to buy anything for the children. What McKay does here is construct a space wherein he articulates, through the vernacular, both the internal and external realities of the Caribbean people. In doing this, he celebrates the identity and practices of a people who had for centuries been displaced and rendered 'inferior'.

Although in 'Two-An-Six' we clearly have the use of a number of words belonging to the English language, McKay here utilizes the Jamaican Creole voice to depict a particular Jamaican cultural scene—market day.

> An' de shadow lef' him face,
> An' him felt an inward peace,
> As he blessed his better part
> For her sweet an' gentle heart.
>   (http://www.poemhunter.com/poem/two-an-six/)

Some have criticized McKay's attempt to use Jamaican Creole in this poem, and it is a fact that there are a number of inconsistencies: he uses very 'heavy' English terms such as 'inward peace' and 'blessed', and later on, 'princely' and 'gnawed', which reveals the inauthenticity of the Creole voice telling this story. There are also moments when the Creole is forced to fit into an English grammar frame, as is seen in the use of the words 'blessed', 'hard-wukd' and 'kissed', where the use of the 'd' is inserted to signal the past tense in English language structure when Jamaican Creole would not have used the 'ed' or 'd' endings as the linguistic marker to represent this tense. Despite the fact that the poetic form McKay utilizes is heavily British however, the insertion of the Creole voice demonstrates an insistence on McKay's part to create a moment that is authentic in its depiction of the Jamaican people. 'In de early marnin'-tide/When de cocks crow on de hill/An' de stars are shinin' still/Mirrie by de fireside/Hots de coffee for de lads/Comin' ridin' on de pads . . . ' Though the Creole voice may seem forced to some, the use of the voice allows a more vivid depiction of the landscape, the food and the culture associated with the Jamaican island.

Also present in the poem is the use of particular Jamaican Creole phrases such as 'soon, soon' ('very soon' in English) in line six ('[s]oon, soon market-people wake'), and 'whole week' in stanza five where the main character has spent 'whole week grindin' sugar cane'. These 'ways of speaking' demonstrate the ways in which the African and European languages have come into contact with each other and have as a result produced a new, authentic language for those existing in the Caribbean. It is the voice of the masses that is represented here in a context that is also a major part of the experience of the masses—market day. It is an attempt to capture the 'flavour' of an experience through linguistic choices that meaningfully contain and embody the cultural practices and emotional realities of the Caribbean people represented in this poem. The male character, for example, makes it clear to the reader the way in which so many people are dependent on him: his wife, children, the labourers he has hired, and the person from whom he has rented equipment—'Ol Bill'.

Once we begin to discuss how Caribbean poetry has transcended boundaries and presented the Caribbean through a language owned, understood and uniquely produced by Caribbean people, we are compelled to turn our attention to Louise Bennett. She demonstrates the value of the Creole voice to convey everyday Caribbean experiences through her use of what was, up until the 1970s, popularly termed 'dialect' poetry. Her insistence on the use of the vernacular in her poetry was based on her desire to represent the realities of Caribbean life for the common folk and the creative ways in which they responded to it. She is important in Caribbean poetry as she gave status and dignity to Jamaican Creole through the way she manipulated the language to produce wise and witty poems that drew on the folkloric practice of storytelling, thereby pulling her readers into her verse fictions. One of Bennett's talents was the ability to produce both humorous and dramatic narrative poems through the use of Jamaican Creole, based on believable Caribbean working-class characters operating in typical day-to-day realities.

For Bennett, the Jamaican vernacular was crucial in depicting the identity and social practices of both the individual and the community in an authentic, 'true-to-life' manner. In her many interviews with both national and international media houses, she expressed the value of the creative power of the Jamaican Creole, particularly in literary representation. Our focus on Bennett will occur through a close examination of the way language has been used in 'Colonization in Reverse' published in *Jamaica Labrish* (2005).

> Wat a joyful news, Miss Mattie
> I feel like me heart gwine burs
> Jamaica people colonizing
> Englan in reverse.
>
> By de hundred, by de tousan
> From de country and from town
> By de ship-load, by de plane-load
> Jamaica is Englan boun.

'Colonization in Reverse' speaks of the 1950s migration experience of Jamaicans to England, after the Second World War, when due to a failing economy and the need for a greater labour supply, England turned to her colonies to help her deal with the labour shortage. In this poem, Bennett 'rewrites' history, demonstrating the irony of the situation where the colonizer has to seek help from the colonized in order to ensure productivity in the 'mother country'. The poem is a clever reversal of the colonized and colonizer relationship which Bennett milks skilfully for sardonic humour. Her inclusion of 'Miss Mattie' provides a conversational tone and communal presence, which reflect the storytelling tradition Bennett consistently utilizes. By merging the oral and the folk in this way, she challenges the primacy of 'the written' and more so the written language of Standard English associated with Europe.

The use of the conversational tone is important when examining language in Caribbean poetry. Through a brief discussion of one of Frank Collymore's poems 'Voici la plume de mon oncle', in *History of the Voice,* Brathwaite suggests that although the actual language of the Caribbean itself might not be present in Collymore's poetry, he disrupts the English-oriented pentameter structure and the rhythm associated with it through a conversational *tone.*

> In a couple of weeks' time school will reopen
>   If not with a flourish of trumpets at least with a shout
>   From the several hundred boys gathered together in the building,
>   And though a few perhaps may wonder what it's all about ...
>   This fuss of education, I mean ... their parents and the others
>   Who have to fit the bill of books and shoes ...
>   (Collymore quoted in Brathwaite, 1984: 32)

Brathwaite argues that Collymore brings to the fore a new way of speaking that has its roots in the oral tradition of the Caribbean people and establishes itself in what Brathwaite terms the 'conversational tone'. So, though for some, Caribbean language solely describes the use of the Creole voice, it is important to note that the presence and use of Caribbean language can also be established and identified through other means, such as the use of the conversational tone. This is also quite dominant in Bennett's 'Colonization in Reverse'. 'What an islan! What a people!', the persona declares in the poem. Bennett's manipulative use of language in this poem reflects the way humour functions in Caribbean society, where people tend to laugh through their misery and suffering, rather than give in to the weight of the burden always hanging around them. Her skilful use of language, sarcasm and humour provides a reflection of this light-heartedness, while still maintaining a serious undertone. In the poem, Bennett speaks subtly about the ways in which Jamaican people were being used by the British. She makes it clear that Jamaicans were misled into migrating to England to work in 'good jobs' and earn 'good money', when upon arrival, they were instead given 'inferior' and 'menial' jobs. Bennett stretches the mockery even further through the 'Jane' who she uses as evidence of the ways in which Jamaicans have turned the joke back on the British by going on the 'dole' and not doing any work at all.

Brathwaite's own poetry in *The Arrivants,* published in 1973, also highlights the use of the Caribbean vernacular to represent the voice and experience of the Caribbean people. In his poem 'The Dust', the presence of the community so evident in Caribbean culture is portrayed through the conversation one speaker has with the other: 'How you? How/you, Evie, chile?/You tek dat Miraculous Bush/fuh de trouble you tell me about?' Here Brathwaite uses Barbadian Creole to affirm the common use of the medicinal practices of the Caribbean people, thereby presenting these practices as authentic, despite the fact that they are often seen as 'uncivilized' compared to the medicinal traditions coming out of Europe. Through the introduction of the 'Miraculous Bush' (which Brathwaite makes a proper pronoun), the reader is able to note the positive effects of this natural, Caribbean remedy. For example, the speaker seems certain that the 'patient' is 'feelin'/less poorly a'ready' and is ' . . . even lookin'/more hearty' having had the bush.

Later in the poem, Brathwaite uses the volcanic dust coming from an eruption in another island as a metaphor to showcase the relationship between the Caribbean islands and to provide a point of focus for the tales offered through the conversations of the women. These tales are told using nation language and are fused together to produce an understanding (the proverbial concept being subtly inserted here of learning from things that have happened) of the way in which sorrow and trouble slowly creep up on individuals, until, like the ashes from the volcano, they manage to darken and destroy everything.

Brathwaite also represents the notion of total expression in this poem; a notion he associates with the oral tradition through its connection with the way in which Caribbean people tend to live—'in the open air, because people live in conditions of poverty . . . because they come from a historical experience where they had to rely on their very *breath* . . . rather than on . . . books and museums and machines' (Brathwaite, 1984: 19). As opposed to the act of reading, which Brathwaite terms 'an isolated, individualistic expression' (1984: 18), the 'total expression' of the Caribbean people comes alive in Caribbean poetry because of the poet's insistence on an audience to complete it. Though this can be detected throughout the poem because of its heavy use of orality, it stands out more effectively towards the end when the voice of the persona seems to be posing a question about life for the masses in the Caribbean, not simply to the other characters in the poem, but also to the audience hearing the poem:

> Dry season follow
> wet season again
> an' the green crop follow the rain.
>
> An' then suddenly so
> widdout rhyme
> widdout reason
>
> you crops start to die
> you can't even see the sun in the sky;
> an' suddenly so, without rhyme,
> without reason, all you hope gone
> ev'rything look like it comin' out wrong.
> Why is that? What it mean?

In this poem, Brathwaite uses nation language and particular ways of speaking that are unique to the Caribbean experience. The common Caribbean-styled greeting opens the poem: 'Evenin' Miss/Evvy, Miss/Maisie, Miss/Maud. Olive,/how you? How/you, Eveie, chile?', capturing the sounds and rhythms of the Caribbean people. It demonstrates the beauty of what would be considered regular conversations among ordinary people and celebrates their way of life by expressing their daily activities and experiences through the use of the Creole voice. Brathwaite demonstrates the way Caribbean language in Caribbean poetry is able to have multiple functions that pull the audience into the many subject matters that arise, such as historical events, herbal remedies, the physical presence of the corner shop, the role of religion in the lives of the Caribbean people and the way it enables a sense of togetherness among the community.

> Hush!
>   Doan keep so much noise
>   in de white people shop!
>
> But yu tek
> it?
>
> Ev'ry night 'fore uh gets
>   into bed.
>
> Uh bet-
>   'cha you feelin' less
>   poorly a'ready!
>
>   I int know, Pearlie,
>   man. Any-
>   way, the body int dead.
>
>   No man you even lookin'
>   more hearty!
>   (Brathwaite, 1973: 62)

The insertion of the Creole voice as representative of the use of Caribbean language is a major feature of Caribbean poetry. Whereas Bennett and Brathwaite write poems entirely in Creole, others may insert only one or two Creole words, idioms or Caribbean 'ways of speaking', i.e. code-mixing. 'Code-switching', described by Pauline Christie as 'the use of more than one language in a single stretch of speech or writing' (2003: 3) is also commonly employed in Caribbean poetry. Such poems may be written predominantly in Standard English but are given a Creole flavour by inserting a Creole word, phrase or sentence.

Lorna Goodison's poem 'The Woman Speaks to the Man Who has Employed Her Son' offers a good example of the Creole insertion.

> Her son was first made known to her
>   As a sense of unease, a need to cry
> For little reasons and a metallic tide
>   Rising in her mouth each morning.
>   Such signs made her know
>   That she was not alone in her body.
>   She carried him full term
>   Tight up under her heart.
>   (Goodison, 1992 : 130)

The term 'tight up' is subtly included as the only example of Creole in this stanza. The use of this term invokes for the reader (particularly the Caribbean female reader), an understanding of not simply the emotional bond but also the physical sensations experienced by the mother who carries a child for nine months.

In her poem, 'My Will', Goodison also demonstrates the way in which certain poets have delineated a distinctive Caribbean space in their poem often through simple, yet profound insertions of a Caribbean belief, proverb, practice or way of speaking. The speaker in 'My Will' uses the conversational tone earlier mentioned. In the line 'May you never know hungry' the word 'hungry' quietly replaces the expected English word 'hunger', thereby subtly introducing a Caribbean inflection to the well-known English proverb and altering the tone of the poem. We note a similar situation in the warning she offers to her son, advising him not to acquire the habit of chasing after money.

> When bindings fall apart
> they can be fixed
> you will find
> that is not always so
> with friendships.
> And no gold.
> Too many die/kill for it
> besides its face is too bold.
>   (Goodison, 1992: 46)

The last line in this section of the poem once again infuses a sense of the Caribbean voice and the way in which Caribbean sayings represent cultural realities. Being 'too bol'-face' is a common Jamaican criticism if an individual was being too forthright or candid. Goodison adjusts this phrase and represents it as 'its face is too bold'. By doing this, she gives a Caribbean flavour to what would otherwise be an English phrase, something the Caribbean reader would be quick to pick up.

The final poem we consider in this chapter is 'Twelve Notes for a Light Song of Light' written by Kei Miller.

> A light song of light is not sung
> in the light; what would be the point?
> A light song of light swells up in dark
> times, in wolf time and knife time,
> in knuckle and blood times; it hums
> a small tune in daytime, but saves
> its full voice for the midnight.
> > (Miller, 2010: 11)

Miller creatively opens up numerous possibilities and multiple meanings for 'light' and 'song' through his fluid use of language. The poem's first two lines are in Standard English: 'A light song of light is not sung/in the light; what would be the point?' And yet, by the fourth line, we get a hint of a Caribbean voice with—'in wolf time and knife time'. The avoidance of the plural for 'time' inserts a Creole inflection and stands out because the rest of the 'note' is written in Standard English. The same situation occurs again in 'Note Eight' where 'a light song of light don't talk' and the speaking voice, previously in Standard English, now drifts into Jamaican Creole. This happens in a natural, easy manner demonstrating of course that many Jamaicans are in fact bilingual, able to use both Standard English and Jamaican Creole equally well.

The inclusion of both languages also demonstrates the conflict the persona seems to face when he finds he has to 'exchange' the language drifting through his mind 'for the ones I think you will understand'. Miller inserts the Creole voice regardless of whether or not it is understood by others, pointing out that when the Caribbean poet is unable to articulate his own voice, what he produces will be 'false'. Miller reinforces the importance of being true to one's own voice and its expression of life experiences and emotions, and states that if outsiders do not fully understand him—too bad: 'tsst/you may not catch everything but chu—/ you will catch enough'. To try to do otherwise, Miller hints, is to try to do the impossible. The poem invites Caribbean poets to feel 'free' to express themselves, to embrace and feel a sense of pride in their own poetic voices.

Miller is careful to establish that '[a] light song of light is not reggae,/not calypso, not mento or zouk,/not a common song from a common island,/not a song whose trail you have followed for umpteen/years', making it plain that his poem is not to be confined to a particular genre of sound, neither is it to be judged as wanting because of how difficult it is to 'place it' or 'define it' or restrict it to some particular label. The very essence of a 'light song of light' resists trite classification; it seeks to represent honestly the tongue of the Caribbean poet, without attempting to adapt to 'ways of speaking' with which an international audience is familiar. Miller could be said to be creating a distinct form of Caribbean poetics. The use of the word 'light' can also be linked to the Rastafari religion, where it becomes seen as an inner light, offering direction, fighting against oppression, negativity and evil. Miller inserts a Rastafarian presence several times in the poem, speaking of 'righteous living', for example, a term commonly used by Rastafarians, and he includes a Rastafari blessing at the end of the fifth note, 'Jah guide and protect always.'

Most powerfully, Miller's artistic use of language documents a people's will to survive in spite of a history borne out of poverty and suffering. Phrases such as 'the thin bellies from which music could be drawn', and the suggestion that these songs were birthed through the price 'of history and cane/and the terrible breadth of oceans: a price/which, even now, you cannot fully consider . . . ', resonate painfully for readers. The symbolic language and authentically Caribbean way of speaking, create a space that encourages reflection on specific cultural realities experienced by the people of the Caribbean.

The language of Caribbean poetry can therefore be represented in numerous ways. It can be identified through the Creole voice, the choice of vocabulary, the folkloric traditions inscribed into the poem's content, the presence of an implicit audience, the distinctly Caribbean images used to convey specific impressions, the plurality of languages, the dominance of orality, the sound and rhythmic patterns, the syllabic presentation of language and the infusion of African and Caribbean language structures and sensibilities. This list of course is not exhaustive as Caribbean poets continue to add new and varied ways of representing the Caribbean.

Teaching the language of Caribbean poetry

When attempting to teach the language of Caribbean poetry, it is important that students be allowed to 'experience' the language, rather than simply be told 'how' the language operates or what the various words and phrases mean. In order to ensure that this occurs, teachers who are attempting to both instruct and engage their students with the language of Caribbean poetry need to take into consideration the definition and features of nation language as well as the history of language and its uses within the Caribbean region. Brathwaite's ideas on nation language are important and help to offer a theoretical framework for particular Caribbean poems.

Students also need to be given the opportunity to hear the language whether it is being presented solely through the Creole voice or through a mixture of Caribbean language-uses or ways of speaking fused together to offer particular sounds and meanings. In addition to this, it would be helpful also to provide students with the opportunity to listen and respond to past interviews conducted with Caribbean poets such as Derek Walcott, Louise Bennett, Kamau Brathwaite, Olive Senior and others. Some of these interviews can be found on the internet so teachers may not have to purchase them. YouTube has many interviews with Caribbean poets that are useful. If the students are at a beginner or intermediary level, then the teacher could listen to these interviews first, then put the information into more accessible formats. For example, graphic organizers where an illustrated map outline of the Caribbean could be used in conjunction with an image of one of the island's key poets above or within it. Students could then place information, such as the poet's views on language, within the frame of the mapped island.

In this chapter, we have emphasized a number of differences in the way language is presented by poets from the different islands. Teachers will find Caribbean poetry much more comprehensible if they have even a basic understanding of the history and culture of the territories connected to the poetry they are exploring. Though there are numerous texts that will speak specifically of Caribbean histories, once again teachers will be able to find a number of resources containing this information on the internet by simply using the Google search tool and typing in key terms. Teachers might also want to look through some of the texts cited as references for this chapter.

It is helpful too that, when looking at the language of Caribbean poetry, teachers recognize and help their students to understand that the use of Caribbean language in and of itself is a move constructed in and through resistance and rebellion. So when Caribbean language or nation language is encountered, attention should be given not only to how it delivers the meaning but also to the value and significance that can sometimes be identified through the mere use of particular words or uses of language.

What is also necessary in the study of the language of Caribbean poetry is to avoid simply trying to analyze the meanings embedded within the use of particular words, phrases, or thoughts, presented through the Creole voice or vernacular, or through Standard English. It is important to be alert to context in the poetry. Teachers should provide opportunities in the classroom that require students to examine how the language of the Caribbean has been defined, how it functions, and also how its expression and rhythm are used to represent aspects of Caribbean life. This might take the shape of listening to recordings of particular Caribbean poems and assessing their similarities and differences; participating in dramatizations or role-play activities highlighting the differences and similarities between Caribbean poetry and British and American poetry (traditional and current); becoming familiar with historical realities and significant individuals who are represented in many Caribbean poems; and looking at the quality and style of the writing.

These recommendations should not in any way suggest that Caribbean poetry cannot be understood without heavy background information. Many Caribbean poems can be interpreted through a first or second reading. What this chapter seeks to do, however, is to help both teachers and students to have a deeper understanding of some Caribbean poems, particularly those that may, at first glance, seem simple and light-hearted.

Chapter 3

Poetry and Caribbean music

Aisha Spencer with Sharon Phillip

Music in the Caribbean is central to its culture, crafted out of the personal and social experiences of its people, and hugely influential beyond its own region. Music has also been used to represent and inform Caribbean realities both locally and internationally. Although Caribbean music existed in various forms and for varied purposes during and after slavery, the shape it began to take in the 1930s and onwards is what we will focus on in this chapter, including the contribution it makes to the understanding of the region's history, identity and potential. Like Caribbean music, Caribbean poetry also became visible during this period, when the quest for a Caribbean identity and the need for more authentic representations of Caribbean experiences began to emerge. The focus at this time tended to be scribal and the major influence was British literature. Much of the poetry of the early–twentieth century, written by poets such as Jamaican-born Claude McKay and Una Marson, Guyanese-born Walter MacArthur Lawrence and Barbadian Frank Collymore, tended to use English models and cadences reflecting British-framed sensibilities that could not meaningfully represent Caribbean landscapes and cultures.

'Songs were the Caribbean's first poems, [but] for a long time, poets limited themselves to the standard ballad style of the Anglo-Scottish tradition' (Brown et al., 1989: 3). By the 1970s, however, the oral tradition in the Caribbean began to influence its poetry in a very different way. Many poets seized the opportunity to communicate more meaningfully with their audience via oral poetry rather than simply through print. Poets such as Kamau Brathwaite, Paul Keens-Douglas and Louise Bennett (though she became known for her poetry after the 1950s and often used the iambic tetrameter quatrains associated with English hymns and ballads) encouraged writers and audiences to acknowledge the deep-rooted relevance of the oral tradition (the use of folklore forms such as the slavery work songs, chants, hymns, calypsos, mentos, reggae songs and games) in the creation of a particular kind of aesthetic for the Caribbean poet. Kwame Dawes (2008) explores this in his work on reggae music (discussed later on in this chapter) focusing on the sound and meaning represented by Caribbean poets who have used the oral tradition to inform their poetry. They have 'made immediately accessible a virtually limitless range of prosodic, rhetorical, and musical shapes, which inevitably [have become] the basis of new making' (Brown et al., 1989: 2).

This chapter therefore demonstrates the poetic ways in which Caribbean music, i.e. calypso and reggae, is used creatively to convey a better understanding of Caribbean realities and the development of new poetic forms and expressions. It looks at a number of songs that can be appreciated as poetry and explores the kind of aesthetic these songs promote. It also explores some of the ways the calypso and reggae sounds coming out of particular islands have influenced the shape and substance of poetry across the region, providing an alternative historical perspective as well as alternative poetic possibilities to the dominant English models—with dub poetry as the primary example.

Calypso: the heart of the beat

The calypso emanated from Trinidad and is considered to be the oldest song-genre in the Caribbean. Calypso delivers political and social commentary and is almost seen as one of Trinidad's institutions of democracy. It first became known for its light-hearted, humour-invoking rhythms, which were fuelled through the sound of the steel pan and lined with the call and response technique.

During the 1930s, with the onset of nationalism and the desire of the West Indian colonies to gain freedom from colonial rule and represent themselves, calypso tents were set up across parts of Trinidad to house demonstrations of protest. These were often subject to police raids, presumably due to the authorities' fear of the political commentaries gaining a wide audience. The presence of these tents and the pan yard (where the steel pans were made and where bands would practise prior to Carnival) became extremely influential in the formation of a particular type of musical and cultural experience. Out of these tents grew the popularisation of calypso and later on, towards the early 1980s, the style known as 'rapso', which was a merging of calypso and Black American rap.

Like some other forms of Caribbean music, calypso began as a genre of protest about life in general and more specifically the politics of the day. It first utilised the conventional arrangement of the kalinda and the picong. The kalinda was the traditional song that used to be sung during stickfighting, while the picong (derived from the French word 'piquant', which means 'stinging or insulting') was the term used to describe the common warlike chants that used to occur between singers 'in the early days' (Warner 1999: 14). Both of these types of singing evolved into the calypso, which, according to Rohlehr (2004), became a medium through which the people celebrated, criticised, applauded, offered their adoration and devotion, challenged, encouraged, provided humour and sent out alert messages. In fact, so comprehensive was the calypsonian's range of topics that one could gain extensive insights into the social, political and other aspects of society of any given period through the music. This trend, which began when the calypso art form emerged, has continued into the 1990s and beyond. Examples include Sparrow's 'Federation', which chronicled the failed attempts to maintain the West Indian Federation that was formed in 1958 and had dissolved by 1962 and Ras Shorty I's song 'Watch out my Children', which warns the youth about the dangers of illegal drugs.[1]

Calypso as poetry

Due to its complex, clever and economical manipulation of words and ideas, calypso is worthy of being seen and valued as poetry. Though the melody is clearly a very important component of the calypso, it is important to note too the significance of the sound of the words and the lyrical content to understand its artistic value. The ballad, Warner states, 'has evolved into one of the main forms of contemporary calypso' (1999: 39). The use of stanzas followed by a chorus or refrain that typically has a specific pattern, and the heavy use of rhyme and metre, also enable the calypso to be read as poetry. In fact, metre is often at the centre of the calypso, holding both lyrics and melody together, often using AABB or ABAB patterns. The presence of voice bends and pulls the sound of the words to produce a powerful aural effect. Though calypso songs are now published printed and in some cases studied, calypso could always be described as being 'part of [a] nonscribal material "litera-ture"' (Warner 1999: 3), based on the characteristics to which it was attached. In looking at how the calypso has informed the crafting of Caribbean poetry, we need to appreciate its different elements, including the important role of the calypsonian. Innovations of form and performance come out of a particular Caribbean aesthetic that has been moulded by the elements and practices of the calypso, such as the oral tradition, the insistent rhythms and the use of humour.

The presence of humour is an important element in calypso. As Breiner (1998) pointed out, humour as a means of relief from life's struggles is an integral element of calypso music, ranging from the absurd, to jokes about social mores and events. The lines may be delivered in a comical manner but with an undertone of seriousness, encouraging people to laugh at themselves, and at the same time reflect on what is being 'sent up'. The humour refers to society's taboos, such as to sexual encounters, race relations or politics. Beneath it often lie serious concerns about the social and political realities facing the Trinidadian people. Inter-national events capture the attention of the calypsonian. One example pokes fun at British royalty. Sparrow's 'Phillip, my Dear', is a comical account of an intruder in the Queen's bedroom, based on a real event.

> Phillip, my dear, last night I thought was you in here
> Where did you go? Working for good old England,
> Missing out all the action. My dear, do you know
> There was a man in my bedroom wearing your shoe,
> Trying on the royal costume, dipping in the royal perfume
> ...
>
> *Chorus:*
>
> He big just like you but younger
> He thick just like you but stronger
> He *lingay*[2] like you but harder
> ...
> He *laylay*[3] like you but badder
>
> (http://guanaguanaresingsat.blogspot.com/2011/10/
> phillip-my-dear-man-in-de-bedroom-song.html)

(Incidentally, Sparrow performed this hit for the Queen at Buckingham Palace some years later!) The joke suggests that a mere commoner is 'better endowed' than Prince Philip. Spar-row demonstrates that even the highest office in the land is not immune to being the subject of the calypsonian's craft. Fun is being made of the white male by the black male and, at another level, the repression of Trinidadian society by the British. The song also shows how calypsonians construct lyrics based on both local and international situations.

Famous Calypsonians such as Spoiler, Trinidad Rio and Funny have also created songs that border on absurdity and irrational actions. Funny's 'Time Really Flies' is a classic example of this type of humour: 'Day before yesterday was yesterday yesterday/Yesterday was today yesterday/Today was tomorrow yesterday/Tomorrow today go be yesterday/Day after tomorrow tomorrow will be yesterday'. Similarly, Paul Keens-Douglas in 'Jus' Like Dat' describes a 'mad' carnival moment:

Yesterday
Ah was mad mad, mad mad,
Mad mad, mad!
Stark ravin' mad!
Yesterday
Ah take off me shirt
An' ah wave it like ah flag,
Jus' like dat!
Jus', jus', jus', jus',
Jus' like dat!
. . .
Den ah crush it, like ah paper-bag,
Jus' like dat!
Jus', jus', jus', jus',
Jus' like dat!
                (in Brown et al., 1989: 43)

While the words and lineation court the rhythm of calypso and celebrate carnival, there is also a sense of futility that occurs after the fun has ended. The 'bawling' and 'wining' and 'jumping' that accompanied the laughter and enjoyment, are by the end of the poem, mere memories and the persona is left to contend with the despairing reality that 'Yesterday was Monday . . . / Yesterday was Tuesday . . . / Today is Wednesday . . . Ash Wednesday,/Jus' like dat . . . O' God!' (ibid.).

Another popular element of the calypso can be identified through the work of the acclaimed calypsonian, Spoiler, in his song, 'Bedbug'—that of the figure of the exploiter, particularly where it concerns human relationships. There are a number of levels of meaning in this song but let us focus on the figure who, having been exploited, desires to seek revenge. Calypso also includes a 'long tradition of anti-feminism' and calypsonians who wrote between the 1940s and 1950s seemed to place their aggression and anger towards the society that was failing them, on the 'plane of male-female relations' (Rohlehr, 1970: 73). In Spoiler's 'Bedbug' we see clear evidence of this.

Yes, I heard when you die after burial
You have to come back as some insect or animal
Yes, I heard when you die after burial
You have to come back as some insect or animal
Well if is so, I don't want to be a monkey
Neither a goat, a sheep or donkey
My brother say he want to come back a hog
But not Spoiler, I want to be a bedbug
Just because . . .

Chorus:

Ah want to bite them young ladies, partner
Like a hot dog or a hamburger
And if you know you're thin, don't be in a fright
Is only big fat woman that ah going to bite ...

The animals introduced in the song are commonly tied to negative stereotypes: the monkey was for many decades seen as being an example of primitive man; the donkey is known as the beast of burden; and the hog is seen as a filthy animal that is ugly and undesirable. The bedbug, however, is believed to be one of the most amazing insects when it comes to sexual prowess. It is constantly mating, has a large number of partners and great virility. Some bedbugs were actually thought to have bi-sexual tendencies and so later down in the song, Spoiler quickly discounts male bedbugs!

We have to bear in mind when examining this song that sex was and still is a popular subject for calypso, not solely because of the typical male/female association, but more importantly because it represents a taboo subject—and at the heart of calypso is the unapologetic intention to address explicitly those subject matters that are otherwise deemed socially unacceptable. In like manner, when Spoiler exalts himself as 'King Bedbug the First', it is not simply a boast, but more a declaration that upon his return instead of being a working-class man chained to poverty, he will hold the title of king and possess all he desires. Unfortunately, the woman is being used as the victim to be exploited and Spoiler envisions himself as her tormentor, so the one exploited will in turn exploit. Interestingly, despite typical patriarchal notions in Caribbean society, the persona wants to be a lowly bedbug after he dies and is reincarnated, not what one might expect of a male afforded a privileged and dominant position in his society. In fact, it speaks volumes about the position working-class men occupy in Trinidadian society, including the fact that it would be highly unlikely for him to engage in intimate relationships with middle- or upper-class females. The word 'bed' is played on throughout the song to connote this idea of sexual contact. As frivolous as 'Bedbug' may seem to many, it is social commentary on the situation of working-class Trinidadian males and how they function in relationships with women. The 'type' of female 'Bedbug' wants to 'bite' are those with money and privilege from the upper classes, prosperity being linked to body weight, the insult thrown out to those who promote injustice in Caribbean society.

If we listen closely to the musical rhythms accompanying the song, we notice the fast paced tempo through which Spoiler delivers his message, suggestive of a male moving speedily from bed to bed and woman to woman. While light-hearted and energetic on the surface, and though quite sexist in sections, the serious issue of exploitation and victimisation within the Trinidadian society is visible beneath the humour. Derek Walcott reprises some of these ideas in 'The Spoiler's Return' (1981) where he includes some of the original song, and emphasises the sound and the message as well. In Walcott's poem, the dead Spoiler returns from 'Hell' to proclaim his message.

I have a room there where I keep a crown,
And Satan send me to check out this town.
Down there, that Hot Boy have a stereo
Where, whole day, he does blast my caiso;

I beg him two weeks' leave and he send me
Back up, not as no bedbug or no flea;
But in this limeskin hat and floccy suit,
To sing what I did always sing: the truth.
Tell Desperadoes when you reach the hill,
I decompose, but I composing still: . . .

I going to bite them young ladies, partner
Like a hot dog or a hamburger
And if you thin, don't be in a fright
Is only big fat women I going to bite.
(Brown et al., 1989: 163–4)

In his poem, Walcott uses the calypso couplet to endorse the satirical and political role Spoiler played as an artiste, creatively speaking on his behalf, and emphasising the culture of a people, even when the messenger has vanished. Walcott gives credence to the worth and relevance of Spoiler's role as calypsonian, promoting the idea that Spoiler's message lives on. 'Tell Desperadoes when you reach the hill,/I decompose, but I composing still . . . ' (see also Chapter 5). Walcott's poem shows how the calypso can be reborn outside of the container and carrier of its original message, enabling new ways of constructing and reading Caribbean poetry through the frame of the musical influences that offer it shape. Brathwaite's 'Limbo' (discussed in Chapter 4) and 'Calypso' quoted below, are two other examples of the calypso influence:[4]

. . . Steel drum steel drum
hit the hot calypso dancing
hot rum hot rum
who goin' stop this bacchanalling?

One of the main features connecting poetry and music is rhythm, which as we have seen is an important element of calypso. The calypso rhythm is not simply the melody and harmony brought out through the sounds of the musical instruments but it also refers to the ways in which the verbal and the musical are intertwined, such as in Sparrow's 'Dan is the Man in the Van'. From its very title, mirroring English reading schemes and nursery rhymes, Sparrow ridicules the British education system that existed in a number of Caribbean territories during colonialism, particularly the people who saw themselves as intellectually superior.

Captain!
There's a traitor on board!
Examine the horn!

According to the education you get when you small,
You will grow up with true ambition and respect from one and all.
But in my days in school, they teach me like a fool,
The things they teach me ah should be ah block-headed mule.

(http://www.maxilyrics.com/mighty-sparrow-dan-is-the-man-(in-the-van)
-lyrics-620e.html)

There are distinct ways in which Sparrow criticises the colonial system of education through the oral version of this song that may not be as evident in the written version. In this calypso, Sparrow seems to be openly scoffing at the ludicrous idea that nursery rhymes will 'civilize' the Trinidadian population.

> Tell me if dis eh chupidness:
> Humpy-Dumpty sat on a wall!
> Humpy-Dumpy did fall!
> Goosey, Goosey Gyander?
> Where shall I wander?
> Ding, dong, dell!
> Pussy in de well!
> R-I-K-K-I-T-I-K-K-I-Ah-T-Ah-V
> Ah Rikki Tikki Tikki Tikki Tavi!
> Dan, is de man, in de van!
> Wepsee mama! Yep!

The written poem cannot reveal the inflexions in voice and variations in pronunciation that intensify the mimicry taking place, but by listening to the oral version of this calypso we are able to hear the ways in which Sparrow satirises the whole situation through peals of his own laughter as he pokes fun at the rhyme. At another point in the song, the intonation lowers, demonstrating both the *low* way those colonised by the British were viewed and, in return, the view of the colonised–of the foolish education system imposed on them.

The mockery can also be noted in the written form, though not as intensely as the oral rendition. For example, we can detect the humorous change of 'Hickory Dickory Dock', which becomes 'Dickory Dickory Duck'. Sparrow shows that he is able to do a better job at crafting his own 'nursery rhymes' by his skilful use of rhyme-scheme and crafting of lyrics that can be freely voiced and yet wrapped within the metrical units presented in the song.

'Dan is the Man in the Van' demonstrates the performative elements of calypso and the ways in which they work together with the political messages embedded in the text. Rohlehr (1970) argues that Sparrow has made a unique contribution to calypso, especially in his powerful use of metre which, according to Rohlehr, is creatively appropriated so as to enable Sparrow to keep 'the rhythms and idioms of Trinidadian speech' (Rohlehr, 1970: 99).

The final element of calypso to be explored in this chapter is the inclusion of the folk tradition. This element is heavily present in David Rudder's 'Haiti' where Rudder, though he depicts a current reality in his calypso, showcases the use of various folkloric forms, such as lyrical ballads, and the act of storytelling. Through positioning the calypsonian as a voice of authority, Rudder offers the next generation a new way of looking at both history and the future. In speaking of the catastrophic earthquake and its aftermath in Haiti, 2010, the song reveals how the calypso can reach beyond its country of origin to deliver a telling message, relevant to the development of Caribbean nations as a region. This 'message' works on an artistic as well as a social level, showing how the calypso is a dominant genre of music and literature in the Caribbean. This is confirmed by Brathwaite's use of Rudder's refrain in the epigraph that precedes his poem, 'Dream Haiti', re-emphasising Rudder's cry on behalf of the entire Caribbean region.

Haiti, I'm sorry
We misunderstood you
But one day we'll turn our heads
And look inside you
Haiti, I'm sorry. Haiti, I'm sorry
One day we'll turn our heads
Restore your glory.

(http://www.davidmichaelrudder.com/Lyrics.php)

Rudder narrates the history of a nation that has endured centuries of suffering and oppression through the lyrical ballad, which is the form utilised by most calypsos, though much associated with the poetry of William Wordsworth, Robert Burns and the like. In Rudder's case, the ballad embodies within it Afro-Caribbean rhythms through the use of the calypso music.

Toussaint was a mighty man
And to make matters worse he was black
Black and back in the days when black men knew
Their place was in the back
But this rebel, he walked through Napoleon
Who thought it wasn't very nice
And so today my brothers in Haiti
They still pay the price ... yeah, yeah ...

The oral tradition of the Caribbean is therefore used to create a new sound form and add new meaning to a form that has existed for centuries. It is also resonant of African culture and connects with calypsonians delivering an apology on behalf of the Caribbean nations. Rudder links the past, present and future through the song's content as well as through the merging of both traditional and contemporary forms of musical instruments.

When there is anguish in Port au Prince
It's still Africa crying
We are outing fires in far away places
When our neighbours are just burning.
They say the Middle Passage is gone
So how come overcrowded boats still haunt our lives
I refuse to believe that we good people
Will forever turn our hearts
And our eyes ... away ...

The sound of the steel pan that merges at points with the drumbeat and the sound of the harmonica, offers a sorrowful feeling even with the presence of a swift beat. It is a rhythm that mirrors the lyrical content of the song, and bemoans the fact that many Caribbean people are still experiencing conditions that existed at the time of slavery. Even with so much happening musically, the song still offers a steady beat and presents a Caribbean voice neatly embedded within the metrical form of the ballad. The steel pan, we must remember, was considered to be a symbol of resistance against white cultural structures and was used to demonstrate the creativity of blacks. This mixture in the rhythmic presentation artfully depicts the sense of disappointment and the apologetic stance of the calypsonian.

Other elements of the oral tradition can be included at this point; storytelling devices and the voice of the calypsonian who speaks on behalf of the people are both present in this song. The latter deplores the continued suffering of the Haitian people and voices the guilt that all members of the Caribbean region should experience as they have not treated each other well. Though his attention is directed to Haiti, Rudder's ballad warns against selfishness, and advises each territory to take responsibility for the fact that some of the conditions of slavery and colonialism still continue today because of the nonchalance of Caribbean people everywhere.

Finally, as the voice of the artist, one who speaks to, and on behalf of his society, Rudder reshapes history and offers a new account of Haiti's past by suggesting that Napoleon Bonaparte, the first emperor of France and one of the greatest military leaders in French history, was in fact wary of Toussaint L'Ouverture, who led the Haitian Revolution and paved the way for Haiti's independence. By doing this, Rudder interrogates the way in which Haiti has been characterised by Europe and seen by other Caribbean territories through what Rohlehr terms the 'narrative, social and political protest' that has emerged from calypso (Rohlehr, 1992: 4).

Reggae: 'revolutionary riddim'

The second dominant musical genre coming out of the Caribbean is reggae music. The emergence of reggae in the late 1960s played a tremendous role in the shaping of identity and national consciousness for the people of Jamaica (and for other Caribbean territories also). The music brought with it feelings of hope and perseverance, the desire to stretch beyond colonial definitions of self, and the need to embrace both blackness and 'Jamaican-ness'. It openly responded to white, Eurocentric stereotyping of Jamaican identity, culture and experience, particularly by post-colonial governments that continued to reinforce situations of prejudice and injustice, despite the political break away from colonial systems of power. The introduction of reggae music opened up a new discourse that allowed artistes to express themselves about the condition of the Jamaican society within the framework of a type of rhythm and beat that spoke for itself with or without the presence of words.

Reggae offers a new way of seeing by capturing the historical and cultural realities of a people and by encouraging a national sensibility that enables people to rebuild levels of confidence and pride, both individually and collectively. Like calypso, but in a different way, reggae music speaks to the condition of the working-class people of Jamaica who continue to face severe poverty, prejudice and various forms of oppression, despite the end of slavery and colonialism. Poets make use of this musical genre. Opal Palmer Adisa draws on this genre in her use of Bob Marley's song 'No Woman No Cry', where she seeks to extend the story Marley begins in his song through her poetic explanation of why Caribbean women don't or perhaps can't cry in her poem 'No, Women Don't Cry'.

> So we women don't cry
> we carry pain
> in our bosom,
> our stomachs bulge
> pregnated by sorrow
> we guard our tears

like a dam
for if we were to shed one drop
we couldn't stop
and we wouldn't have been able
to fight the Portuguese in the Congo,
the English in the Portland hills of Jamaica or
prisoners and derelicts of Europe in the Americas.
(Adisa, 1992: 87)

Reggae not only speaks to the socio-political terrains of life, particularly as experienced by the working class, but it also has 'a close relationship with Rastafarianism, a religious political movement that has transformed significantly the language and culture of Jamaican society' (Dawes, 2008: 56). This relationship was also concretised through Bob Marley who pulled both forms together through his music with songs such as 'Jah Live' in 1975 and 'Give thanks and praises' released in 1983. This spiritual component of reggae is celebrated in Lorna Goodison's 'Jah Music' and Mervyn Morris's 'Rasta Reggae'. It is therefore felt by some that reggae music allowed for 'the spread of the philosophy and language of Rastafari' (Makoni et al., 2003: 69). While Bob Marley is best known, other reggae artistes popular during the 1970s and the 1980s include Peter Tosh, Burning Spear, Bunny Wailer, Black Uhuru and the group Third World.

Reggae and poetry

Kwame Dawes writes 'Reggae is about spaces, about the way sound fills space and then vacates space to create the suggestion of energy . . . [; it is] a quality of sound that evokes a world of experience' (2008: 16). Not only is Reggae music characterised by the presence of spaces, it has also opened up new spaces for many writers, enabling 'a pivotal and defining historical moment in the evolution of a West Indian aesthetic' (14), where the form and content of reggae began to be used by a number of poets in the 1980s onwards as an aesthetic tool with which to sculpt Caribbean poetry through a Caribbean voice, using elements of Caribbean culture, affirming their own language and identity. At this point, we will focus on several features of reggae: the revolutionary voice or rhetoric in the music; the ways in which the past and the present are linked to offer a reinterpretation of a people's experience; its working-class grounding (Dawes, 2008) and its distinct rhythm.

The revolutionary voice or 'rhetoric' that characterises reggae music can be found in Peter Tosh's 'Equal Rights and Justice' and Bob Marley's 'Get up, Stand up', where the artists encourage people to do what the song says and 'stand up for your rights' rather than passively accept that which disenfranchises them. In 'Equal Rights and Justice', Tosh complains in the refrain that 'Everyone is cryin' out for peace/None is cryin' out for justice'. The revolutionary charge can be identified through the demand for equality—in Tosh's case by his firm rejection of the Christian ideology which promotes the concept of 'peace on earth', and in Marley's, through his demand for an alternative to the Eurocentric philosophies to which they have been exposed.

Preacherman, don't tell me,
Heaven is under the earth.

I know you don't know
What life is really worth.
…
Stand up for your rights. Come on!

Marley's speaking voice conveys the discourse of Christian religion as oppressive and reconstructs it to fit into his own Reggae (and Rastafarian) rhetoric, suggesting that it is not through Christianity that the people will find the light but rather in their own story 'that has never been told'. Here we see in action what Dawes terms 'political and spiritual anger and revolutionary activism' (2008: 71). The voice of the artist indicates unequivocally his role in society—to reveal a path where Caribbean, black identity and experience are embraced and used to point the way forward.

The connection between the past and the present is identified in the reggae band Third World's song entitled '96 Degrees in the Shade'. It refers to the 1865 Morant Bay Rebellion to secure freedom led by Paul Bogle and the brutal response of the colonial authorities. The song, which offers an opposing view of history to the typical European version, refers to the hanging of both Paul Bogle and George William Gordon during an October that was said to have been extremely hot.[5] The song rejects the anonymity commonly associated with black people and places it instead on the historical figure Governor Eyre, by referring to the latter only as 'the big fat boy . . . the Queen employ'. Whereas the European version of history celebrates the capture and destruction of two men who were threatening the plantation, Third World offers an opposing notion of that reality: 'you caught me on the loose/fighting to be free/now you show me a noose/on the cotton tree'. Through this song we are therefore offered what Dawes terms 'a poetic narrative of history' (1999), turning the story around so that the label of 'uncivilized' shifts from the black insurgents to the white oppressors. This 'act of historical retrieval' (ibid.) shows how Caribbean people have been shaped by slavery and celebrates the resilience of their ancestors, one of the factors that 'distinguishes reggae and the fact that it speaks to modern Jamaican realities even as it recalls the past is what gives it such a potent immediacy' (Dawes, 2008: 127). The need to remember history as a means of ensuring an awareness of self and as a form of action propelling Caribbean people to continue to move forward, is a constant theme in reggae music. Reggae artistes such as Burning Spear, Luciano and Queen Ifrica portray black history within a number of their songs.

Reggae is central to the sense of self and nationhood held by Jamaicans. It provides an understanding of the historical journey of the Jamaican people, and at times the people of the Caribbean at large, and brings them face-to-face with the interrelatedness of past, present and future worlds. In addition to this, it provides Caribbean writers with an aesthetic within which to inscribe their poetry because of what is embodied within its rhythms and structures. The function of reggae is extremely important. It is the kind of music that impels people to rock or dance because of its complex play of guitar lines or its 'one drop' sound that encourages movement. It is also the kind of music that evokes a deep sense of connectedness between the listener and the individual telling the story. The 'working-class grounding' and the rhythm of reggae can both be identified in Bob Marley's 'Talkin' Blues' with its unmistakable feeling of melancholy, interspersed with anger and frustration. As you listen to the music of this song, the deep sound of the bass guitar pulls you into the experience the singer relates; and the shrilling sounds of the electric guitar could be seen to easily parallel the sound of a human cry at the pain of injustice. As Marley sings, the musical backing gives an impression of wailing, emphasised too by the harmonica. So words and music work powerfully together to declare its message.

Dawes refers to reggae as 'an ensemble musical form that relies on the dialogue between a range of instruments in a way that does not give one instrument privilege over another' (2008: 111). All of the instruments in 'Talkin' Blues' work together dynamically. The singer laments the hardship of life through graphic description of his living conditions—'cold ground was my bed last night/And rock was my pillow too'—and his hopelessness—'I've been down on the rock for so long/I seem to wear a permanent screw', and the sounds of the instruments in the song establish the narrative in a way that the written word on its own could not do. Beyond the suffering, however, the hopefulness so popularly associated with reggae comes through, when Marley asserts that he's 'gonna stare in the sun/let the rays shine in my eyes / . . . take just one step more . . . '—the message is of 'never giving up'. This is one of the key elements of reggae that seems to speak to individuals from diverse cultures across the globe—it rails against social injustice *and* it heals, as it were, through its replacement of the negative emotion with a 'positive vibration'. As one born and raised in poverty in the heart of Kingston's inner city, Marley offers an authentic story of an experience well understood by the masses. Through this song, Marley exhibits 'reggae's capacity to engage in the most profound issues of human existence' (Dawes, 2008: 135). He is not only 'talkin' blues', he is also 'playing blues', demonstrating the capacity of reggae to provide the artistic interlinking of lyric and music.

Dub poetry: in-between 'word' and 'sound'

Dub poetry pulls heavily on the musical features and characteristics of reggae (particularly the character of the DJ, the use of the drum and the use of Rastafarian language) in its presentation. 'The word "dub" is borrowed from recording technology, where it refers to the activity of adding and/or removing sounds' (Morris, 1999: 36). Dub poetry occupies the middle space between word and sound, joining both elements together to produce a distinctive form of Caribbean poetry. It is written to be performed and so dub poets (though some reject the label as limiting and restrictive) usually offer what is popularly known as performance poetry, much of which can also be enjoyed on the page. The performance element is significant as it is connected to the fact that print is associated with Europe, while the spoken and performative is associated with African culture and folklore. Dub poetry, which emerged in the 1970s, has since become an international art form. It is sometimes seen as having a close connection to 'protest poetry' due to its harsh content, which attacks oppression and injustice and often engages in political discourse.

Dub poetry connects the written text and the oral production through Creole, the vernacular, which is used to establish the dub poet's resistance to Standard English. Dub fuses together European and African oral and literary constructs and representations, manipulating language in a powerful way, representing the Caribbean experience while at the same time demonstrating its adaptability through the use of particular European linguistic markers. In offering this kind of fusion, a new and diverse form and mode of expression is created. It is through dub poetry that we understand the significance of evaluating the use of 'sound' in both the language and the music of poetry. Mikey Smith offers an example:

Me sey me cyaan believe it
me seh me cyaan believe it

Room dem a rent
me apply widin
but as me go een
cock-roach rat an scorpion
also come een

Waan good
nose haffi run
but mi naw go siddung pon high wall
like Humpty Dumpty
me a face me reality
one lickle bwoy come blow im horn
an me look pon him wid scorn
an me realise how mi five bwoy-picni
was a victim of de trick
dem call partisan politricks
an me ban me belly and me bawl ...
me seh me cyaan believe it
(in Brown et al., 1989: 37)

The employment of repetition ('me seh me cyaan believe it') and alliteration ('an me ban me belly and me bawl') are two among many examples of the amplification of sound in the language and musical cadences of the poem.

Further, we see the 'writing back' post-colonial response to Western colonial influences and culture on Caribbean life described by Ashcroft et al. (1989). Mikey Smith, for example, contrasts his response to the daily struggle he faces with responses promoted by European solutions, through his refusal to 'siddung pon high wall' (a practice popularly associated with idle Jamaican young males) like the popular English nursery rhyme character, Humpty Dumpty. Like the calypsonians, he mocks and subverts English nursery rhymes by replacing them with references to his own cultural practices.

Smith is one of the best dub poets to analyse when we are attempting to interpret dub poetry. 'Mi Seh Mi Cyaan Believe It' demonstrates how rhythm is used through voice and how both written and oral text can co-exist meaningfully. The rhythm is connected but not restricted to the sound of the reggae beat, shifting in and out, rising and falling, as it blends with the rhythms of speech. The intonations of his performance are matched to the content. For example, the speed with which the daughter's boyfriend gets her pregnant can be heard through Smith's fast delivery of the word 'ship' ('an im pass through de port like a ship'). The repetition of 'me seh me cyaan believe it' dramatises the effect of the daily struggle while the anguish is depicted through the drawn out sounding of particular words such as 'cyaan', 'horn', 'scorn'. The connection between word and sound can be identified through the use of harsh consonants, such as 'cockroach' and 'scorpion', whereas the loud wailing of 'woeeeeee' dramatises the mounting feelings of frustration and fatigue that the persona feels he has had to bear at the constant violence ('Who dead? Harry dead!/Who dead? Eleven dead!/Woeeeeeeee'). The audience is pulled into that moment through the controlled nature of the scream, making a powerful impact on the rhythmic flow of the poem.

Jean 'Binta' Breeze, a well-respected poet, uses some of the same themes in 'Riddym Ravings', a powerful feminist poem. Breeze inserted a strong female voice into the largely male dominated dub poetry scene, opening up female sensibilities otherwise left untapped. In 'Riddym Ravings', the central voice is that of an impoverished, homeless woman with the realities of her life presented squarely to the audience/reader. Nothing is left uncovered, including the mental state of the persona. One of the ways that the Caribbean woman seeks to dislocate herself from the patriarchal constructs within which she is being forced to exist is to assume a state of madness. Through this madness, manifested by her choice of language, rhythm and tone, she is able to reinvent herself and resist the roles prescribed for her by the male.

Breeze wants us to understand that the Caribbean woman stands doubly marginalised. She has to continually fight European notions of racism still resonant in her society, while at the same time having to contend with patriarchal prescriptions of how she ought to behave as a woman, perpetuated by Caribbean males who treat her as a second class citizen. Through her representation of the 'mad' female, Breeze is able to explore female consciousness and portray the social conditions experienced by many Caribbean women who continue to be exploited and silenced. Breeze uses the DJ's voice to emphasise the value of music in the fabric of Caribbean life as it is the music that keeps the persona going, the one thing that society is unable to take away from her. Within the debilitating narrative of her wretched life, the woman breaks into song, articulating the insistent voice she keeps as a radio in her head; 'eh eh no feel no way/town is a place dat ah really kean stay/dem kudda-ribbit mi han/eh ribbit mi toe/mi waan go a country go look mango' (Breeze, 1992). In this poem, Breeze demonstrates how dub poetry rests in the space between word and sound as her 'riddim ravings' tell the truth about the misery caused by injustice, prejudice and the general disregard for lower-class women in Jamaican society.

Teaching Caribbean music as poetry

Allowing students to engage with recorded songs, YouTube and actual performances will assist them in discovering the various connections between rhythm and meaning in Caribbean poetry. Teachers can further students' understanding and appreciation of Caribbean poetry by helping them to see how rhythm is being represented; for example, through the use of drums, polyrhythmic structures, a particular beat or tempo, the strategic use of the persona's voice or the way words are placed together to achieve a particular effect. They need to understand that rhythm is not only confined to music and dance! Students can also be given opportunities to explore the value of music in the representation of reality, the projection of both individual and collective identities, and in the emergence of new ways of reading and writing poetry through the frames of different genres.

In conclusion, students need to understand how music, song and sound inform meaning in Caribbean poetry, articulating a sense of 'Caribbeanness'. Caribbean poets have been successful in capturing the rhythmic potential of poetry, through merging patterns of sound and music with linguistic uses of Caribbean talk, out of which has emerged a unique, indigenous 'riddim poetics'. While the music of Caribbean poetry is popular in many parts of the world, there is still some way to go in gaining wider recognition for what the poetry has to say and for the artistry and complexity of how it says it. Teachers can make a difference.

Notes

1 Sparrow is a very popular performer of calypso who emerged in the late 1950s.
2 Lingay tends to mean of a tall, slim build (more than likely referring to the private part in this case).
3 Laylay refers to one's sexual prowess.
4 From *The Arrivants: A New World Trilogy* (1973: 49).
5 See *The Story of the Jamaican People* by Philip Sherlock and Hazel Bennett (1998).

Chapter 4

Poetry of oppression, resistance and liberation

Georgie Horrell

That the native does not like the tourist is not hard to explain. For every native of every place is a potential tourist, and every tourist is a native of somewhere . . . so when the natives see you, the tourist, they envy your ability to leave your own banality and boredom, they envy your ability to turn their own banality and boredom into a source of pleasure for yourself.

(Kincaid, 1988: 18/19)

For many young people—indeed for many British, European or American people of almost any age—the Caribbean represents a world of leisure, luxury and life at its most exotic. As holiday destinations of choice for the wealthy, the islands of the Caribbean offer idyllic escape from life's stresses—places where one can enjoy rest and recreation . . . whilst gently humming Bob Marley's 'Don't worry about a thing . . . '. Good weather (that is balmy, warm days and nights) is what the fortunate traveller expects, along with 5* hospitality. Unless, of course, you come from one of the many islands that make up the Caribbean, in which case the most obvious notion associated with the West Indies is, simply, 'home'. Whether read 'at home' or elsewhere, however, the poetry of the Caribbean is powerfully evocative. In much of this poetry, the very sound of the language employed is distinctively Caribbean and the images used are often vibrantly allusive to a sense of place (as indicated in the Introduction and Chapter 1). Landscape, seascape, flora and fauna gesture firmly to 'island life' that stands in many ways in direct contrast with the 'island life' of the British Isles. Furthermore—and dissonant with notions of rest and recreation—much Caribbean poetry also engages with a distinctive sense of history, offering particular and in many ways deeply traumatic perspectives on the 'roots' of Caribbean life. This is, of course, history that connects intimately with the history of British, European and American children in ways that they may not immediately recognise. Whether teaching Caribbean poetry to Caribbean children or to children from elsewhere, this sense of history—understanding it and connecting to it—is a vital opportunity for the teacher. As children engage with the poetry and its roots, fresh, illuminating and liberating perspectives are offered. In this chapter, I will consider how the poetry of the Caribbean has the potential to enact what McGillis considers as the core impulse of post-colonial texts:

Postcolonialism as an activity of the mind is quite simply intent on both acknowledging the history of oppression and liberating the study of literature from traditional and Eurocentric ways of seeing . . . The postcolonial writer confronts directly the forces of cultural domination and racial intolerance.

(McGillis, 2000: xxiii)

As many have noted—poets not least—the dangers of 'Eurocentric ways of seeing' are pervasive and persistent both in Europe (and Britain) and in formally colonised places like the Caribbean. As Kamau Brathwaite argued in the mid-1980s:

> Shakespeare, George Eliot, Jane Austen—British Literature and literary forms, the models which had very little to do with the environment and the reality of non-Europe—were dominant in the Caribbean Educational system . . . People were forced to learn things which had no relevance to themselves.
>
> (1984: 8)

Calling the Caribbean a 'cultural disaster area' (and likening the situation in the Caribbean to that of other formally colonised regions such as South Africa) Brathwaite insisted, 'we are more excited about their literary models, by the concept of, say, Sherwood Forest and Robin Hood than we are by Nanny of the Maroons . . . ' (ibid.). While it might be noted that writers and poets like Brathwaite have of course changed people's cultural perspectives through their work, there is none the less a legacy of Eurocentrism that prevails in many parts of the world—and in the Caribbean no less. Marlene NourbeSe Philip writes eloquently in her poem 'Oliver Twist' of schoolgirls in Tobago who regard themselves as 'a cut above [their] parents', absorbing British culture and learning British history, 'learning about odes to nightingales/forget hummingbirds . . . about princes shut in towers/not smelly holds of stinking ships' (Philip, 2005: 334). Education systems exported to the West Indies had school children in Jamaica reading and writing about snow and daffodils—and more insidiously, thinking about their own language and culture as in some way inferior to that of Great Britain (Brathwaite). Olive Senior's poem, 'Colonial Girls School' similarly describes how 'Borrowed images/willed our skins pale/muffled our laughter . . . Told us nothing about our selves/There was nothing at all' (Senior, 1985).

The poems cited in this chapter open opportunities to think about the 'history of oppression' in the Caribbean and how the trajectory of Caribbean history from slavery to a post-colonial moment may be traced. This continuing enactment of the history of the Caribbean is explored here primarily through four poems, suggesting how critiques of racism and injustice—past and present—permeate the poetry. The horror of slavery is always there in the background but so too is an on-going interrogation of the conditions for marginalised peoples in a globalised world.

For both Caribbean and children from elsewhere, the post-colonial impulse in much of the poetry of the Caribbean provides a means of opening up a journey of transformation. In her book, *Radical Children's Literature: Future Visions and Aesthetic Transformations in Juvenile Fiction*, Kimberley Reynolds considers how literature encountered by children and young people contributes to the 'social and aesthetic transformation of culture by . . . encouraging readers to approach ideas, issues and objects from new perspectives and so prepare the way for change' (Reynolds, 2007: 1). And Beverley Naidoo similarly points out that:

> Literature has the tremendous quality of allowing us to engage imaginatively in the lives of others. It enables us to move beyond ourselves and our own experiences. If we allow ourselves to respond to it fully, it can be a great educator. For those of us brought up monoculturally, literature which springs from outside our own boundaries can be a life-line.
>
> (Naidoo, 1992: 16)

Caribbean poetry offers teachers the opportunity to throw their pupils a 'life-line', as Naidoo suggests—pulling them out of blinkered or narrow ways of thinking and offering them an opportunity to view themselves and their culture in fresh ways. Perhaps, more than anything else this is precisely because young people are offered a view of the past from another, challenging perspective.

Kamau Brathwaite's 'Limbo' is a well-known (and often taught) poem that draws together the conflicting sensibilities alluded to in the opening to this chapter: both the tourists' view of Limbo—a rhythmical dance performed with athleticism and extreme suppleness—and Limbo as referencing a perilous state of in-between-ness—the space between Heaven and Hell—are suggested here. The poem keys into a sharply significant set of historical events.[1] The torturous use of human bodies in the practice of slavery is clearly suggested, as 'Limbo' describes the Middle Passage, endured by the men and women captured in Africa and taken to work on the plantations owned by Europeans. 'Limbo' is an evocation of that terrifying journey as they were held and taken 'between' continents in the most horrific conditions. John Agard similarly plays with the multivalent notion of 'Limbo' in his 'Limbo Dancer at Immigration' (1985). The contrast between a contemporary (Western) view of the islands as places of relaxation and pleasure, and harsh historical reality is brought into stark focus in both these poems.

Brathwaite's poem evokes the driving rhythm of the limbo dance, repeating 'Limbo' and 'Limbo like me' throughout. The poet draws on the sounds of the Caribbean as expressed in the rhythms of the music that would accompany limbo dancing—but the rhythm also gestures towards a 'deeper history' of African roots. Thus, the ironic tensions—of tourist entertainment underwritten by a history of displacement and oppression—are expressed in the sound and experience of the poem read aloud. The somewhat relentless, compelling rhythm—the single sentence poem (there is just the single full stop at the end of the poem) driving and pushing towards the almost cathartic, yet also ominous, final lines: 'hot/slow/ step/on the burning ground'—carries the sense of inescapable destiny experienced by the slaves. The poem simultaneously suggests both the compelling joy of the dance and the unavoidable hell-like horror of arrival for the slaves in the 'New World'.

Indeed, for young people this is often read at first as a poem that is 'fun' to read and easy to perform. Of course, there is much that lends itself to classroom drama and expression and while a glib encounter with the poem's potential as entertainment would certainly represent a missed opportunity, allowing pupils to experience the vibrant, persuasive pulse of the poem is a way into the deeper implications of the lines. Readings accompanied by percussion, particularly drums, would be appropriate and effective. Furthermore, the poem suggests something of the 'griot' (storyteller) experience, of call and response, with lines repeated, these repetitions answering, underlining and emphasising each 'storyline'.

> long dark deck and the water surrounding me
> . . .
> limbo
> limbo like me
> . . .
> stick is the whip
> and the dark deck is slavery
> limbo
> limbo like me
>
> (Brathwaite, 1973: 194–5)

Thus, in a call and response reading, the poem imaginatively evokes the collective experience and suffering of the slaves as they make their way from the lost 'Heaven' of their homeland to the 'Hell', the 'burning ground', of the islands of the Caribbean. Here they would labour on sugar, cotton and tobacco plantations, effectively building on their whipped backs the wealth of Britain and Europe.

Much Caribbean poetry engages with this terrible history, drawing as Brathwaite does, the links between the past and the present—demonstrating the enduring imprint of such a past on the lives of twentieth and twenty-first-century island people. Edward Baugh's 'Sometimes in the Middle of the Story' is another such poem. Here, Baugh is writing from the perspective of a descendent of slaves, sensing the ever-presence of the past. He directly engages with the notion of the storyteller telling a tale that somehow invites ghostly inter-ruptions from this troubled past. Something 'outside the house', apparently outside the community of the present but yet profoundly related, stirs and reminds the company of its presence. This 'outside' figure is both victim and revolutionary. Toussaint Louverture is evoked—the Haitian slave leader who defied Napoleon and established a free, independent black state. The poem celebrates Toussaint as a hero with extraordinary powers, describing him as:

> on his grey horse Bel-Argent, moving
> faster than a backra-massa timepiece
> know to measure, briefing the captains
> setting science and strategy to trap the emperor.

The figure of Toussaint engages with modernity (he sets 'science' as well as 'strategy' to 'trap' Napoleon) as well as with something outside European knowledge: he is able to travel faster than the white oppressors' and slave owners' means of keeping time are able to measure. The sense of folktale is recreated in this poem—but it is a tale told both distinctively (note the use of Jamaican: both in syntax, 'but is not the wind' and vocabu-lary 'backra-massa', blended with 'standard' English) and—with the sense of the ghostly voices of the murdered dead—harrowingly. Because, if Toussaint is passing, he is coming 'from secret rendezvous, from councils of war' with those ghostly men who did not sur-vive the Middle Passage: 'their souls shuttle still'. The poem becomes not only a memorial to a hero, but also a memorial to the Africans who were deliberately drowned *en route* to the West Indies—whose lives were spilt to balance slavers' books against insurance claims. Speaking with the ghostly voice of an ancestor, the narrator describes the questionable survival of a slave below decks:

> and we below deck heard only the muffled
> thud of scuffling feet, could only
> guess the quick, fierce tussle
> the stifled gasp, the barrel-chests bursting
> the bubbles rising and breaking, the blue
> closing over.

Furthermore, the evocation of these drowned Africans becomes an ominous, perhaps threat-ening, sense of potential power to be unleashed against oppression—past and present.

> the ebony princes of your lost Atlantis
> the power of black men rising from the sea.

The poet suggests that the community evoked at the opening of the poem, those listening to the story, are also intimately linked to these drowned people—that the lost souls still 'shuttle', 'connecting' those living in the present in a dynamic way with those who were sacrificed. Indeed, their horrible deaths become a source of 'power' to fuel both Toussaint's rebellion and a sense of a necessarily resistant identity in the present. The poet directly addresses and draws in the community listening: it is a message for 'us' and the princes are 'your[s]'. It is precisely the acknowledgement of the past, both heroic and tragic, which will empower and equip the people of the present.

The notion that 'History' is a powerful tool for creating individual and communal identity is also exercised in John Agard's poem, 'Checking Out Me History' (2007, Poetry Archive). Here too, the poet evokes past Caribbean heroes—Toussaint, Nanny the Maroon[2] and Mary Seacole[3]—juxtaposing these (along with references to the early inhabitants of the Caribbean, the Arawaks [Taino] and Caribs, as well as African [Zulu] leader, Shaka) with European—or rather Eurocentric—historical figures. The accusation is clear: 'Dem tell me . . . but dem never tell me' implies a clear colonial policy to present a superior, more 'important' history that omits and overshadows histories of colonised peoples. The implications for people living today are made obvious by the poet when he concludes, 'I carving out me identity'. What this poem demands we consider is the notion that there are multiple histories to be told—and that for many people, living in the UK as well as in former colonies, the key to a robust sense of identity is an understanding (and validation) of their past.

There are at least two areas of interest that teachers may explore in relation to this poem. The first is the implicit idea that education is effective and non-oppressive when it allows young people to engage with knowledge that is genuinely meaningful. In Agard's poem it is perhaps the information that is not provided—in other words, that which is silenced—which is significant. The poem in fact becomes a short history lesson in itself, gesturing to alternative and resistant histories that the reader may well be tempted to explore. Pupils may be encouraged to do some research themselves—on the figures Agard mentions or on figures that feature in histories significant to their own particular backgrounds. Discussions concerning the manner in which history is constructed and the question of who 'gets to tell' the 'official' history of a group of people, would be fruitful.

The second area of interest that Agard's poem opens up is the idea that 'identity' is bound up with knowing about our histories. Pupils could be invited to think about this and to write poems 'checking out' their own histories. As Agard aptly writes in a Guyanese creole-influenced voice here, pupils may like to play with using an English indicative of their own use of dialect. The connection between language and identity is made explicit in much Caribbean poetry (see Chapter 2) but teachers might like to point out that there are of course many variations of English, some perhaps more subtle than the Caribbean variants but no less significant as markers of particular identities.

Much of Agard's poetry celebrates a sense of resistance to oppression: resistance to cultural dominance (represented as much in the content and in the language and form of his poetry), resistance to past colonial oppression (as in the revolutionary figures referenced in 'Checking Out Me History') as well as resistance to present manifestations of injustice (as suggested in 'Limbo Dancer at Immigration'). Other Caribbean poets similarly engage with past colonial wrongs in the light of twentieth and twenty-first-century injustices. Olive Senior's (2005) 'Meditation on Yellow' is a poem that sweeps across the wrongs of Caribbean history to arrive at a troubled point in the present and concludes with a wistful gesture to the future. The poem most particularly draws a line from the slavery burdened past of the Caribbean to a commercialised tourist present. The political economy of the Caribbean is teased out in a manner that suggests a historical continuity between the days of slavery and the place of much of the Caribbean in a globalised present.

Despite the restful, contemplative state perhaps suggested by the title, Senior's poem is one of tensions: between past and present, between the vernacular languages of the Caribbean and Standard English and between (former) colonist and (formerly) colonised. Indeed the poem's power lies in part in its play between contemplative—apparently gentle—lyricism and playfully ironic, but pointed critique. Furthermore, the ambivalent manner in which the Jamaicans view tourists is brought into sharp focus here. The dislike and 'envy' of tourists expressed in Jamaica Kincaid's jeremiad[4] (from which the quotation is taken at the opening of this chapter) is translated into firm dismissal in Senior's verse. The speaker in this poem draws a connective line between the colonists of the past, who traded 'a string of beads/and some hawk's bells' for 'a string of islands/and two continents' and the tourists of the present, who 'arrive' 'just when [she] thought/[she] could rest' (2005).

> And just when I thought
> I could rest ...
> a new set of people
> arrive
> to lie bare-assed in the sun
> wanting gold on their bodies
> cane-rows in their hair
> with beads—even bells
>
> So I serving them

The speaker here moves into a hint of Jamaican—'I serving'—ironically underlining both her difference from the visiting Westerners and the role of servant that she once again finds foisted upon her. Her reference to 'a new set of people' is a distinctively Jamaican expression which deftly, subtly, creates a sense of 'us and them'. Rhyme in these lines emphasises her description of a practice that is deliberately nostalgic of Empire, with the 'civilised' taking of tea:

> At some hotel
> overlooking the sea
> you can take tea
> at three in the afternoon
> served by me
> skin burnt black as toast
> (for which the management apologises)

And here the speaker moves from her gentle acceptance, her easy accommodation of the visitors and firmly, but with the weight of history in her voice, insists:

> Though I not quarrelsome
> I have to say: look
> I tired now ...

For one day before I die
from five hundred years of servitude
I due to move
From kitchen to front verandah

Throughout the poem, the speaker connects with a history of exploitation, speaking at first from the perspective of the Tainos and Caribs (the original inhabitants of the islands), as well as from the perspective of slaves brought from Africa ('I've been travelling long/cross the sea . . . slaving in the cane rows/for your sugar') and concluding in a post-colonial voice of one whose time has come to reclaim the right to their own recreation and rest:

I want to feel mellow
in that three o'clock yellow

Where does the tourist—or neo-coloniser if you like—stand in relation to Senior's poem? The speaker in the poem tells them to 'lump it or leave it'—a neat reversal or alteration of the usual British phrase that instructs the hearer to 'like it or lump it'. 'Liking it' is implicit, a given perhaps—and no longer on offer. Rather than being permitted to take on or to 'colonise' Caribbean 'style' ('cane-rowing' their hair and wanting it 'dread'), the speaker points out the fact that 'you cannot catch my rhythm/(for you have to be born with that)'.

However, despite the clear expression of rejection of exploitation and commensurate affirmation of desire, the final line of the poem is wistful, hopeful and not wholly assured—and perhaps suggestive of one who is wearily pessimistic, or at best only tentatively optimistic. For rather than claiming the rest she is due, the speaker points out that 'You cannot reverse/Bob Marley wailing' and rather than *taking* her seat on the 'verandah' (vocabulary aptly borrowed from a distinctively colonial lexicon: Verandah [1711] is borrowed from Hindi [varandā] via Portuguese [Britannica Online Encyclopaedia, accessed 9 May 2013]), at 'three o'clock', she sighs that she will do so 'any day now'. Here it seems that Senior claims Marley's voice as representative of the significant historical intervention that Jamaica Kincaid, in her work, postulates is the missing factor for inhabitants of the Caribbean. In *A Small Place* Kincaid says, 'They [the inhabitants of Antigua] have nothing to compare this incredible constant with [that is, the heightened, intense moment of every day in beautiful Antigua], no big historical moment to compare the way they are now to the way they used to be' (1988: 56). Kincaid suggests a fortunate/unfortunate ahistorical present which locks the 'natives' of Antigua into a trap of unreality, marginality and servitude within the tourist industry: an enforced passivity. Olive Senior's poem pushes towards a more promising, open future marked by—or ushered in by—the distinctive and deeply challenging sounds of a global phenomenon (Marley). This intervention, the poem demands, cannot be 'reversed'.

Olive Senior's evocative and provocative poem thus takes into account a terrible history and resists the perpetuation of oppression. Her poem challenges the ways in which Caribbean people have had their identities framed and marginalised by discourses of servitude. 'Colonial Girls School' hints at a reversal of cultural domination as Senior optimistically concludes, 'One day we'll talk about/How the mirror broke/Who kissed us awake/Who let Anansi from his bag/For isn't it strange how/northern eyes/in the brighter world before us now/Pale?' Anansi—the folk character or trickster—is invoked to indicate a liberation from the Eurocentric imposition of the past and an ability to look (despite the erstwhile oppressors' 'northern eyes', which are now simply 'pale') to a brighter future. However, in 'Meditation on Yellow' historical slavery (the poem suggests) is extended into a global side-lining of the Caribbean whereby peoples who had everything taken from them in the past now are valued only in the way in which they might entertain and serve the privileged of the West. Of course this is done in a manner ironic and lightly humorous, in a poem also richly allusive to the cultural and geographical life of the Caribbean. While the poem may be fruitfully explored by tracing the speaker's voice (allowing pupils to think about the way in which the 'I' at first speaks from one historical era but then moves through time to a modern moment), Senior's poetic techniques invite creative and thought provoking responses from pupils. For example, the colour yellow is evoked throughout, referencing 'gold' (set in opposition to false and deceptive gold as well as to cold silver—the 'glint of your sword', the 'bullet'), the warmth of the sun, the yellow of fruit and plants and a number of other suggestive associations, in a manner imaginative and creative. Pupils might be encouraged to think about a colour that they would associate with their countries, geographical areas or cities and then, similarly, play with the ideas this engenders in the writing of their own 'meditation on . . . '. Another approach might be to write a poem drawing on cultural markers as Senior does, in order to reflect on cultural identity: as opposed to the sun, lemon grass and Bob Marley, British children might think about rain, fish-n-chips and the Beatles.

The poets considered in this chapter meet McGillis' criteria for a post-colonial approach: they 'acknowledge history[ies] of oppression' and in diverse ways they work to liberate 'the study of literature from traditional and Eurocentric ways of seeing' (2000: xxvii). Further-more, by opening up possibilities to understand something of the histories in which Caribbean poetry is rooted, these poets offer ways of equipping teachers and pupils to 'confront directly the forces of cultural domination and racial intolerance'. For the non-Caribbean reader, the 'cultural tourist', Caribbean poetry seldom permits an easy, unexamined reading but rather pushes the reader—albeit with wit and humour—towards a more critical perspective of their own position and purpose in the world.

Notes

1 The Atlantic triangular slave trade existed from the sixteenth to the nineteenth century. Carib-bean crops such as sugar and tobacco, grown with slave labour, were shipped to Europe to enrich colonials and provide the funds for manufactured goods. These were then used for the continued importation of African slaves transported along the sea lane known as the Middle Passage. Millions of people were enslaved and many died, but the Atlantic slave trade was an extremely lucrative practice.

2 Nanny was a legendary slave leader, who led a group of runaway slaves in Jamaica (the Blue Mountains area). Nanny and her brothers became folk heroes, some sources suggesting that she freed more than 800 slaves over a 30 year period (Government of Jamaica, National Heroes listing, accessed 1 March 2013).

3 Mary Seacole (1805–81) has been voted 'Greatest Black Briton'. Born in Jamaica, Seacole served as a nurse in the Crimea – after being rejected four times by the organisation of Flor-ence Nightingale. Setting up the 'British Hotel' at her own cost, in the heart of the battlefields, Seacole defied racism and proved both her courage and her skill (Anionwu, 2006).

4 A prolonged complaint.

Chapter 5

Understanding and teaching Walcott in two settings

Velma Pollard and David Whitley

Velma Pollard from the University of the West Indies (UWI), Mona, and David Whitley from Cambridge University, UK, jointly planned but separately taught a unit of work on Walcott's poetry in Jamaica and Cambridge, respectively. This chapter shares the process of poetry selection, as well as some teaching strategies and insights that might assist teachers in their practice.

Preamble

A surprising number of teachers of Caribbean literature regard Derek Walcott's work as difficult and so shy away from introducing it to students. This is a pity, especially since younger Caribbean poets are producing excellent sophisticated poetry, which might in turn get equally ignored unless we manage to change attitudes. This 'unit' is an introduction to Walcott focusing on the Caribbean landscape/environment and Caribbean people. Walcott is unashamedly passionate about both as his work continuously illustrates. The selection of poems is meant to underline the variety of ordinary concerns the poet addresses, the simple elegance of his craft and his interaction with music, including the popular rhythms of the region. The time recommended is not enough to do justice to these aims but this introduction hopes to be careful enough to encourage readers towards a continuing relationship with Walcott's work.

Teachers who avoid Walcott's poetry say it is complex, yet a considerable amount of Walcott's output is written in very simple language. Deeper questioning usually throws up the accusation that the allusions included in many of the poems make them inaccessible. The age of technology makes such a claim invalid. There is no reference in a Walcott poem on which Google cannot throw light. Our aim is to demystify Walcott's poetry and to help teachers make him accessible to secondary school students.

Some background information may be useful to explain why Walcott's allusions are difficult for this generation of readers. Walcott is a product of his schooling. He studied English Literature and the Classics as part of what he himself labelled 'a sound colonial education'. When he came to the University College of the West Indies, Mona (then UCWI-London), requirements for entrance to the university included a pass in Latin at high school level. Those classical and other references that seem obscure now were a natural part of the information that his cohort would have learned. Students of later years used to spend hours in extensive research to understand some of the parallels he drew. With the advent of search engines, however, research involves only a click on the mouse.

Another presumed difficulty may have to do with the selection of poems. In any enterprise it is foolhardy to ignore the significance of pace. It is important where you begin and how you continue. As teachers we need to remember that it is possible for us to choose poems in such a way as to engage students meaningfully. In this chapter we pay particular attention to selection, beginning with simple poems and moving to the more sophisticated. Three of the poems we have chosen are included in an early edition of an anthology of Poetry for Caribbean Examinations (Pollard, 1980) so there is the confidence that the poems can be accessible to students at that level.

This chapter describes the interaction between presenter and participants over a selection of Walcott's poems taught on both sides of the Atlantic, to mainly Bachelor of Education student teachers at UWI and practising teachers on a Continuing Professional Development course in Cambridge.

The Caribbean experience

Teachers may have access to a video clip of Walcott responding to an interviewer in the 1980s and talking about Caribbean writing against a backdrop of Trinidad. That video is useful as part of background information. Walcott is a man of the outdoors, chiefly the sea. In the poem 'Schooner Flight' in *The Star-Apple Kingdom* (1980), he has Shabine (arguably himself) say inter alia 'I'm just a red nigger who love the sea . . . ' There are people in this video clip: the descendants of enslaved Africans and indentured Indians, some of whom still live in depressed circumstances on hilltops or near canefields. He reads an excerpt from a poem named after a poverty stricken hillside of Port of Spain, 'Laventille'. It is that hill to which he refers in another poem 'Spoiler's Return' (discussed in detail later in the chapter) where the calypsonian Spoiler, returning from the dead, sends a message to Desperados steel band, which traditionally rehearses on that hill: 'I decompose/but I composing still'. One of the ironies of the situation Walcott writes about is that sweet music comes over the hill from ugly poverty. It might be interesting and certainly instructive to read his Nobel Prize acceptance speech published as 'The Antilles: Fragments of Epic Memory' (Walcott, 1998). It uncovers much of what he thinks and how he feels about the Caribbean: indeed, his thoughts about the collection of people wonderfully thrown together in one location are relevant here. The city is in Trinidad but the history is the same in most of the islands. He writes of a people 'that cannot be subdued by slavery or indenture' (70).

> They survived the Middle Passage and the *Fatel Rozack*, the ship that carried the first indentured Indians from the port of Madras to the canefields of Felicity, that carried the chained Cromwellian convict and the Sephardic Jew, the Chinese grocer and the Lebanese merchant selling cloth samples on his bicycle . . .
>
> And here they are all in a single Caribbean city, Port of Spain, the sum of history, Trollope's 'non-people'. A downtown babel of shop-signs and streets, mongrelized, polyglot, a ferment without a history, like heaven. Because that is what such a city is, in the New World, a writer's heaven . . .
>
> (70–71)

Selections and process

The following poems were selected for the Jamaican students' teachers: 'Midsummer Tobago' and 'Oddjob, a Bull Terrier' (*Sea Grapes*, 1976); 'As John to Patmos' (*In a Green Night*, 1969); 'The Light of the World' (*The Arkansas Testament*, 1987). The session begins with a video clip of Walcott talking to an invisible interviewer with people and nature forming the backdrop. (Any of the many interviews with Walcott now available on YouTube may be used here though the richness of the visual background would be lacking.) The intention is to present a simple relaxed artist talking about his life and his work.

We begin with a clear reading of 'Midsummer Tobago' by a good, forewarned reader or a recording available on the internet. This allows for an appreciation of the sound, the pace of the poem and the economy of the words. After one or two readings it is time to look at it on the page. An interactive session follows as together we lift image and meaning from the sparse effective words on the page and appreciate the depth of meaning Walcott puts into a few lines. There are small debates over specific lines. We reach consensus by finding cues in the poem to support decisions. Participants vary. What one group catches immediately, another does not. A case in point is the 'green river', part of an experience of drought recognizable by readers from one island, difficult for those in another where there has never been drought enough to have green moss on stones where water should be flowing. The cues are there but different experiences affect the ease or difficulty of access. The first movement of the poem is made up of images of heat in Tobago in summer. Other Walcott references to summer heat come to mind from 'Another Life': 'Days/ the sun drumming, drumming,/past the defeated pennons of the palms/roads limp from sunstroke . . . ' (1973: 53) and in 'Port of Spain' from *The Fortunate Traveller.* 'The oven alleys stifle/where mournful tailors peer over old machines/stitching June and July together seamlessly' (1982: 61).

Walcott and his family lived in Trinidad for many years. You may have heard cynics say that the beaches of Trinidad are in Tobago so spending part of the summer with your family in Tobago is a common practice. The second movement of the poem is nostalgic and philosophical:

> Days I have held,
> days I have lost,
>
> days that outgrow, like daughters,
> my harbouring arms.
>   (1976: 83)

In terms of the selection of syntax, we can appreciate the present perfect (perfective) in the first two of those lines. It is a past looking over its shoulder at what so recently was the present. In terms of meaning, it is the quick flight of time rendered here in a way that can be considered anything but hackneyed. In the lines that follow, we allow ourselves to be touched by fathering and what Walcott makes of it. The cliché about fathers and the special love for daughters, whether myth or truth, finds a place here.

Parents who watch their children become adults can relate to 'outgrow' and the nostalgia and almost regret that goes with it: the kind of ambivalence parents feel about 'losing' children. We spend some time on the phrase 'harbouring arms'. A man who loves the sea writes of 'harbouring arms'. A simile might have made the overtones more obvious. Why does he not use that device? It is anybody's guess. Perhaps the advantage of brevity? But we understand the comparison anyway. The description 'safe harbour for ships' comes to mind. A kind of calm comes over the room as we appreciate this simple poem and give it a final reading out loud.

The next poem 'Oddjob, a Bull Terrier' is to be absorbed on an emotional level only, not dissected in any way. It is a comment on loss by death of dog, child, friend. Read aloud its effect is palpable. This poem moves everybody.

> You prepare for one sorrow,
> but another comes.
> It is not like the weather,
> you cannot brace yourself,
> the unreadiness is all.
> (1976: 85)

Each participant finds a personal moment that relates to some aspect of it. It is very different from the earlier poem. Walcott is a poet of many moods. He contrasts 'unreadiness' for sorrow suddenly thrust upon us with 'readiness' for natural phenomena such as storms that give some warning. Are there echoes here of Hamlet's expression of fatalism in 'readiness is all' and his last words at the end of the play: 'The rest is silence'? Over and over, Walcott admits his debt to those who wrote before. In a recent discussion in Jamaica (May 2012), he mentioned that Pasternak said that great writers have no time to be original. As Edward Baugh says of Walcott: 'His view is that all poets benefit from other poets, and that it is the contemporary privileging of originality that should be questioned' (Baugh, 2011: 93).

'As John to Patmos' is the second poem in *In a Green Night*, a collection of early poems written between 1948 and 1960. It expresses Walcott's passion for and total commitment to the Caribbean. It is a kind of mantra. He swears that he will love forever all its people—'The living and the brown dead'. You may want to explore the placing of the adjective that must qualify both living and dead. How else could he have placed it? Was rhythm the predominant reason or was it just an error? Walcott himself has spoken about the sometimes virtue of a typographical error. Could it have been 'the brown living and brown dead'? Why are the people brown here and 'black' earlier in the poem? One response to that may be that when slavery is mentioned, the connotation of the word 'black' is usually used, but 'brown' is more commonly used to describe Caribbean populations in general.

In the same participatory fashion as with the Tobago poem we work this through but with surprisingly little excitement. Yet it is an important affirmation and a continuing one in the life of this poet. You might have to go to the Bible yourself so you can explain to your class who John is and the importance of the isle of Patmos in his life so the full import of this long simile can be appreciated. You may want to point out the geographical similarity between two strings of islands, archipelagoes, one Greek the other Caribbean. It is a comparison that recurs in Caribbean literature not only in Walcott's work. David Whitley points us to 'Another Life', Walcott's first long poem and the more extensive expression of his feeling. He and his painter friend make a pact (and here again John seems to be the point of departure) 'that we would never leave the island/until we had put down in paint in words/ . . . every neglected, self-pitying inlet' (1973: 52).

By the time we get to 'The Light of the World', longer and more complex than any of the poems we have read so far, it is surprisingly accessible. To introduce it we listen to Bob Marley's 'Kaya', the song whose first three lines form the epigraph for this poem, which then begins: 'Marley was rocking on the transport's stereo/and the beauty was humming the choruses quietly.' It is a poem about the poet feeling like an outsider on a minibus from the village, Gros Islet to Castries, the capital city of St Lucia. We compare and contrast Marley and Jamaica with Walcott and St Lucia at that time. Marley sings 'I feel so good/in my neighbourhood', while Walcott feels alienated from his.

The class becomes alive and indicates where we should break the reading and begin the discussion and when we should resume the reading. The poem is long and requires a break. The point has to be made here that Walcott has been a painter as long as he has been a poet, though he has spent far more time on the latter pursuit. You will have to tell your students this and point to the painter's eye and its response to people in the minibus, particularly a beautiful young woman who he compares to a famous painting. (You can find a copy of the painting to which Walcott refers on Google: 'it was like a statue, like a black Delacroix's/*Liberty Leading the People* . . . '.) Participants quickly pass that over this time to identify the response of the poet-man with whom they are well pleased. Reader Response Theory has something to offer here about the reader and the text.

The poet-painter would put good gold earrings in the ear of this woman who wore no jewellery and highlight certain aspects of her face. The poet-man later puts a white night-gown on her and wishes to follow her to their imaginary house on the beach and lie down beside her. He looks carefully and long at this woman but she does not return the gaze. She keeps her head down because it is impolite to look at strangers. And he is a stranger there as much as he does not want to be. He describes her in great detail and inwardly exclaims: 'O beauty, you are the light of the world.' This is an image used to describe himself and his friend Gregorias in 'Another Life' but apostrophized and in this context it has a different ring. It is an outcry that may indeed be related to any number of classical elements in Walcott's experience but may equally be related to 'lyrics' from the ordinary Caribbean man who does not resist the impulse to praise a beautiful woman in hyperbolical terms. The most extravagant of these I have heard goes: 'Moses must have been sleeping when one like you leave heaven.' Walcott resists the urge to voice his thoughts but he does want to tell her extravagant things, such as that he: 'would buy her Benin if she wanted it,/and never leave her on earth'. Note how in a quick all-embracing after-thought he includes all the passengers in the people he does not wish to leave: 'But the others too'. You may want to tell your class that art in bronze from Benin, Nigeria, is world famous and that they can see photographs of pieces on the internet.

'The Light of the World' explores themes of exile, abandonment, rejection. Descriptions of the people from whom the poet feels alienated are clear (such as the face and the house of the beautiful young girl) and they may come with their own language, which is not the English language of the poem. The older of the popular languages of St Lucia is a French Creole. A woman with extra luggage wants to be taken into the transport going into the city, Castries. She is struggling to get herself and two baskets on to it. She fears that she will not make it. In her panic she shouts to the driver: '"*Pas quittez moi à terre.*"' Walcott makes use of her need and exploits the linguistic nuances of her cry. He translates it to English first as, '"Don't leave me stranded"', then repeats the request and sees the historical moment as a common one: people like her have always been left stranded. He becomes philosophical and translates that cry in a number of ways sometimes changing the stress: '"Don't leave me on earth" . . . "Don't leave me the earth [for an inheritance]"' and finally '"Don't leave me on earth, I've had enough of it."'

To watch Walcott work that line with its nuances and alternatives is to watch at work a master from a multilingual society. Be sure to allow your students to see all that he makes the lines do and follow him to the end of the poem where the abandonment is total when the packet of cigarettes he leaves on the bus is returned to him, illustrating the people's honesty but interpreted by him, in the context of his mood, as proof that these people want nothing from him. When he alights from the transport, his outsider situation is reinforced by the fact that he leaves for a hotel, ironically named the 'Halcyon Hotel', while the other people in the minibus are going home. The poem ends: 'There was nothing they wanted, nothing I could give them/but this thing I have called "The Light of the World".'

The British perspective

The unit on Walcott's poetry that we produced for teachers in Britain had considerably less time allocated, so we had to adjust the material we had developed for the Teaching Caribbean Poetry course. This section, therefore, offers some additional reflections on how we tried to inflect the course towards a British cultural context in terms of pedagogy and material. We started, as in the Mona version, with 'Midsummer Tobago' to emphasize how Walcott can use straightforward, accessible images and language to powerful effect. Two further dimensions came into focus in relation to this poem, though, which you may find it useful to think about. First, many teachers were very interested in developing creative responses, offering students a chance to write parallel or responsive versions of Walcott's verses, centred on their own experiences and sense of place. The apparent simplicity of 'Midsummer Tobago' made it seem very amenable to this kind of approach. The first part of the poem consists purely of a sequence of images, enabling a particular scene to be made present for the reader. The images might be understood to function as descriptions of place, epitomizing something essential in the experience of Tobago in midsummer, or as evocative of a particular mood. One aim in terms of asking British students to write their own sequence of images would be to understand how the same technique could create a range of emotional effects and responses in their own, different contexts. Another aim would be to deepen understanding of parallels, as well as contrasts, in approaching poetry from another part of the world.

Another thing we noticed was that the poem, even though very short, seemed to change its direction, tone and point of view in the second part. Whereas the first part of the poem is characterized by images of a particular place experienced in the context of intense heat, the second section is reflective, making more generalized comments about the speaker's perception of time. The verses here have a quite different feel. The immediacy and presence of the initial images seem to act as a prompt to take up a much longer view of life as a whole. The diction changes here too, picking up a distinctive rhythm with the repetition of 'Days I have . . .'. Teachers who went on to use this poem as a model for a particular kind of creative writing with their pupils found that pupils often imitated this rhythm and phrasing at the end of their own poems, producing a parallel range of meditative effects. One could argue that the poem itself embodies some of the qualities of older traditions (derived from both oral and religious culture) enabling the rhythmic repetitions at the end to have particular gravity and force. Recognition of such deep roots within older cultural forms may contribute towards understanding how such an apparently simple poem can become so moving. A teacher could easily ruin this effect by directing attention towards technicalities too early: pointing out to students, for example, how the second part is rhetorically structured, as 'anaphora'. This may create an abstract distance before the full experience has been allowed to deepen and mature. An alternative strategy, though, would be to offer comparable experience of language that has affinities to Walcott's expression here, and works in similar ways. For instance, students might be asked to read—or listen to—part of chapter three from the Book of Ecclesiastes, in the Bible.

> To every thing there is a season, and a time to every purpose under heaven;
>   A time to be born, and a time to die; . . . a time to embrace and a time to refrain from embracing;
>
> A time to get, and a time to lose;

To listen to a passage like this is to become absorbed by a pattern of rhythms and contrasts that set off archetypal human experiences against each other—time and change, procreation and loss—developing a profound feeling for the connectedness of all things within the music of time. Many readers may feel there are parallels between the patterned alternation of 'A time to get, and a time to lose' and Walcott's 'Days I have held,/Days I have lost'. The biblical passage is not necessarily a direct source, but experiencing it alongside Walcott's poem may help embed a primal, rocking rhythm fully in the ear and, in turn, enhance appreciation of the apparently effortless power and grace of Walcott's closing passage.

Although we also looked briefly at one or two of the other poems Velma Pollard has referred to, we decided to devote a more substantial amount of time to 'The Spoiler's Return', when teaching the course in Britain. This poem, which pushes calypso rhythms into the mould of traditional English iambic pentameter couplets, offers a vivid, lively sense of much that is distinctive in West Indian culture. But it is also positioned in a hybrid way, in between expressive traditions of the old and new worlds, and works well as a kind of bridge enabling deeper engagement with the context of Caribbean poetry for students in Britain. The liveliness of the poem—the speaker's voice imitates a kind of carnival performance—and the appeal of its animating conceit, are both central in this regard. Young listeners can respond readily to the idea of a rakish, popular performer returning from the dead (where he has been residing in Hell) to sardonically goad his fellow Trinidadians for their moral and political backsliding.

The poem adopts the persona of one of the most famous of all calypso singers in the Caribbean, the legendary 'Mighty Spoiler', whose real name was Theophilus Philip (1926–60). Philip was perhaps the most influential of the generation of calypso singers who achieved fame after the Second World War. In the course of his brief, alcohol fuelled, and, in many ways, chaotic life, he composed some of the most memorable lyrics in the calypso tradition. Walcott recalls the figure of Spoiler from the dead in a spirit of irreverent homage, honouring the popular performer's legacy by investing his revenant voice with a mixture of biting mockery and big hearted wit that suggest parallels with Shakespeare's Falstaff. Indeed, this is a poem of large ambition that plays off the tongue-in-cheek 'mightiness' of its star persona from humble roots. The poem operates by turns as cultural critique (it is a mordant assessment of the state of the nation), as a railing sequence of philosophical aperçus that strip humanity of its pretensions, and as a bold exploration of affinities between a popular art form still owned by the poor and the revered classics of literary satire. The Spoiler's exposition concludes by graciously acknowledging his debt to the tracks laid down by his mightier literary antecedents: 'names wide as oceans when compared to mine/salted my songs, and gave me their high sign'. But, for the duration of the poem, the stage is Spoiler's alone, as, through him, Walcott reclaims the high calling of the poet's voice across the ages for the most downtrodden people of the Caribbean.

This brief review may make the poem sound too challenging for using with a class of fifteen year olds but, in fact, the speaker's voice is grounded in ordinary particulars throughout and, once the initial hurdle of strange vocabulary and range of references is overcome, the poem is both very accessible and great fun. The multiple references both to topical, local issues and to historical parallels ranging across many different countries are a potential barrier initially, and we will return to consider strategies for dealing with the breadth of allusions later. But the poem has so much going for it, in terms of its potential to engage students at many different levels, that it is well worth taking on these difficulties.

One teacher, who works in quite a tough area in Tottenham, North London, was immediately attracted to the idea of getting his pupils to write their own versions, substituting a figure from one of the London gangs they knew for Spoiler coming back from Hell to upbraid and warn his contemporaries. Certainly the sense of being immersed in a state of corruption that is both bodily (the Mighty Spoiler's own physique is memorably imagined as 'decomposing' in the process of 'composing' his lyrics) and characteristic of a whole society gives the poem a stance—or 'attitude'—that is potentially appealing to the young. Moreover, the couplet form, which might appear offputtingly traditional in another context, is actually one of the easiest poetic modes to imitate (though not with Walcott's consummate skill and range obviously). It is the basis of popular culture song modes such as rap and hip hop, which adolescent listeners in most countries within contemporary culture will have heard extensively. So there is a strong, natural base to build from here.

So how do we deal with the range of references? First, we are appending a set of footnotes to this chapter that provide brief explanations for most of the references and should save enthusiastic teachers some leg work. The pedagogic issue though, is how to make the references interesting, enhancing the poem rather than weighing it down. There are three things to bear in mind that should help with this. First, a good many of the references are topographical and will only come alive if the reader has developed some sense of the places to which the poem refers. Right at the heart of the poem is the Laventille, an impoverished community with poor housing and a bad reputation that lines the slopes of a hill overlooking Trinidad's capital city, Port of Spain. There are plenty of pictures of Laventille available on the internet, together with news video footage of periodic shootings and protest riots that have taken place there in recent years. Although it is important not to create a simple negative stereotype as counterpart to the tourist images of the Caribbean, selective use of this imagery can forge an initial understanding and sense of connection to the poem's setting, out of which deeper understanding and interest can grow. Once this is established, the local words used in the poem—like 'limeskin' and 'shirtjacs'—can be understood and identified within context. 'Limeskins' are hats that have become floppy and can be pulled down over the eyes to give the wearer a bit of style and attitude (or hide identity from the authorities). Classes with adolescents will all have equivalent items of 'street fashion' and drama activities could increase the sense of connection.

Second, many of the references embody instances of gross injustice or illuminate corrupt political practices. Once the reference is grasped, it can grow into debate about the underlying ethical or political points involved and animate the young's generally keen sense of social justice. The word 'bohbohl'—meaning bribery or corrupt practice—reverberates across the whole poem, for instance. But this also feeds into a wider, more complex ethical territory in terms of the politics of the developing world. Spoiler is keenly aware in his tirades that, since his death, Trinidad has benefited financially from the discovery of substantial oil resources within its territory. Sections of its population have become rich, as a result, whilst others remain desperately poor. Spoiler also raises the question of what a resource rich country in an impoverished region should do with its wealth more generally. He draws a scornful picture of other countries coming to Trinidad with metaphorical begging bowls in their hands.

There is room for lively debate on general issues here that can quicken responses when the class returns to the poem.

Finally, the classical references could seem simply 'learned' in another context. But here they are drawn in side by side with reference points in ordinary, popular culture all the time. Walcott runs a lively quote from the famously loose living seventeenth-century poet, Lord Rochester, into lines from Spoiler's own most famous calypso song 'Bed Bug'. Exploring some of these references in more detail can bring dead names and their preoccupations to life in a contemporary context, enriching understanding of the poem's texture whilst pleasurably enlarging students' sense of their own intellectual reach.

For those seeking additional material that is engaging and powerful, we would also recommend the following poems, which are available with a reading by Walcott himself on the Poetry Archive website. 'Blues' (1969) is one of Walcott's most accessible poems and should engage young readers readily from early secondary school stage onwards. It appears to be written in the manner of Langston Hughes—a conversational voice with a light touch on a serious subject matter, involving racial discrimination and violence. The speaker reminisces about an occasion on which he was beaten up by youths in New York because he is black. The poem has a curious tone though, that might well spark off interesting discussion and further exploration. While not exactly resigned to the situation, the speaker's attitude seems to be one of 'toughing it out', including quips and off-beat kinds of ironic commentary, that seem to invite neither easy sympathy nor conventional protest. He seems to be focused as much on preserving his smart new jacket as on enduring or surviving the encounter, for instance, and finishes with a sardonic sounding joke about tough love. The tone of this poem is less straightforward than appears at first and well worth opening out for more extended discussion.

'Sea Canes' (1976) is more difficult than 'Blues', but opens similarly, in a disarmingly straightforward, conversational mode (that oddly manages to sound formal at the same time) with the line—'Half my friends are dead.' The lyric meditation on death, loss and re-affirmation that follows is metaphorically rich and allusive, but also surprisingly clear, strong and memorable in its conclusion. Resisting the sentimental urge of memory to embellish and idealize those we have loved and lost, the speaker cleaves fast to a more stringent, truer vision of the dead 'as they were,/with faults and all, not nobler, just there'. The quiet, but firm diction shows a poet working at the height of his powers, transforming the language of ordinary speech into a testament of faith in that 'poor, bare forked animal', man (as Shakespeare put it in *King Lear*).

Although the speaker's situation may be distant from that of young readers, we are all bound by the common thread of mortality and loss, as Velma Pollard's earlier comments on 'Oddjob' make clear. The way 'Sea Canes' works to sustain its central faith and commitment to those whose life force can only be recovered through the imaginative power of memory is similarly stirring. There are opportunities here to explore the resonances of haunting lines such as 'float with the dreaming motion/of owls leaving earth's load', as well as to encourage appreciation of the inner strength of emotion that is restrained as well as expressive. As the great American poet, Emily Dickinson, once put it: 'After great pain a formal feeling.'

For more advanced groups, the themes of the poem might be productively engaged with through consideration of distinctive elements in its form. Why does Walcott shift the uneven line lengths of the first four stanzas into a much more regular, ten syllable, iambic pattern in the last three verses, for instance? What does this more formal patterning do for the stance the speaker takes up here? And why is the pattern loosened (just a little) in the last 9 syllable line, where the quietly insistent 'there', at the end, fills up the whole space of an iambic foot on its own? What is the effect of starting with a quatrain and finishing with a couplet? And of the mixture of full and half (imperfect?) end rhymes? These ways into considering the effect of the poem through subtle details of its distinctive formal variations will only work for some classes. What should be available for all, though, especially with Walcott's reading to ground appreciation in the ear, is the richly modulated and compelling quality of this meditation on the most fundamental aspect of experience binding all humans together—our shared mortality and our capacity to love.

Conclusion

Walcott is the only poet who has been given a complete chapter in this book. This is less because he is the only Nobel Prize winning poet in the Anglophone Caribbean than because of the need to help change the response to his work which we noted in the preamble to the chapter. If our discussions help in any way to make this poet's work seem more accessible and serve to give some teachers the confidence to take his work into the poetry classroom, then our intention will have been served.

(Additional) Notes to accompany 'The Spoiler's Return'

Page numbers refer to *Derek Walcott Collected Poems 1948–1984* (1987).

p. 432

Dedication—'for Earl Lovelace': Caribbean writer whose novel, *The Dragon Can't Dance* (1979), reflects on aspects of calypso culture in contemporary Trinidad.

'Laventille': poor district in Trinidad's capital city, Port of Spain. Contains an area known as 'Hell's Yard'.

'rum-eaten wit': Theophilus Philip, aka 'Mighty Spoiler', died of alcohol-related diseases at the age of 34 in 1960.

'limers': dialect word for idlers.

'peel my limeskin back': 'limeskin' is a dialect word for an old hat that has gone floppy and can be pulled down over the face. 'Peeling' the hat back means that the Spoiler's face, now decomposed, can come into full view.

'a dead macajuel': dialect word (pronounced 'makawell') for a boa constrictor or anaconda.

'caiso': calypso.

'Desperadoes': a Trinidadian steel pan orchestra (the British Queen mother is reputed to have had their records and listened to them!).

'the hill': a significant part of the district of Laventille is pitched on the side of a hill.

'*I going to bite them young ladies* . . . ': the Mighty Spoiler's song, which won him the 'Calypso Crown' in 1953, is a multilevelled satire and bizarre fantasy. The speaker imagines being re-incarnated as a bed bug after death, which enables him to bite women in their sleep. The tone of the song is rendered more complex by the way it weaves issues of social distinction into this conceit. The singer will only bite 'big fat women', who will have more flesh for him to feed on than their undernourished, working-class counterparts. The upper-class pretensions of the big, fat women become a target for the song's satire in the process.

However, the singer also singles out women of this class and stature because, through them, he sees a route towards climbing socially himself, attempting to achieve 'nobility' vicariously through the promiscuous sucking of their blood, till he can crown himself 'Bedbug the First'. There are perhaps some distant echoes of Robert Burns' 'To a Louse' in terms of the way the central conceit is worked here.

p. 433

'shirt-jacs': loose fitting (generally short-sleeved) shirts worn outside the trousers.

'Rochester, who praised the nimble flea': Rochester's 'Satyre Against Reason and Mankind', whose first four lines Spoiler quotes verbatim in the italicized passage that follows, contains no reference to fleas, though it does share with Spoiler's poem the fantasy of being reincarnated as an animal ('dog, monkey or bear') after death. Walcott seems to be conflating Rochester with John Donne here, and invoking Donne's famous seduction poem, centred on the image of a flea biting two would-be lovers. Walcott seems to play fast and loose with his persona's textual references on occasion—as Chaucer does with the Wife of Bath's citations—and the resulting textual instability is no doubt a deliberate effect.

'I hope when I die . . . ': this couplet is the 'chorus' from 'Bed Bug'; the poem invites Lord Rochester to join in with Spoiler's calypso ('join Spoiler' chorus'). Rochester's own lines at this point continued:

> I'd be a dog, a monkey or a bear,
> Or anything but that vain animal
> Who is so proud of being rational.

V.S. Nightfall: a jibe at the famous Trinidadian novelist, V.S. Naipaul. Naipaul is often criticized from a post-colonialist perspective, accused of writing with a pessimistic edge that is ultimately derogatory towards the cultures of developing world countries and too complicit with the values of the developed world. Walcott actually has much in common with Naipaul, and deeply admires many aspects of his art, but is also sharply critical of these tendencies. The 'area of darkness' allusion also represents something of a 'poetic slippage', since *An Area of Darkness* (1964) is the title of Naipaul's first non-fiction book about India, rather than 'The Middle Passage' (1962), which is a travelogue and cultural critique of the Caribbean. The 'darkness' image fits the persona's poetic intentions better here though.

'dasheen': a large round, edible tuber.

'hearing aids . . . dark glasses': Dr Eric Williams, a notable Caribbean historian, was the first Prime Minister of Trinidad and Tobago in 1956, remaining in post till his death in 1981. He was famous for wearing dark glasses and had a hearing aid, which he was reputed to turn off during his comparatively infrequent visits to parliament in his later years.

p. 434

'crown and mitre me Bedbug the First': see earlier comments on Spoiler's calypso song.

'mordant': biting (a standard English word, of course, but pupils may not know what it means).

'bohbohl': large-scale fraud and corrupt practices, carried out by well-placed persons in companies or government.

'they say that Rodney commit suicide': Walter Rodney was an eminent historian of the Caribbean region, and a political activist on the left. He was assassinated in 1980 by a car bomb while running for office in Guyana.

p. 435

'Attila' . . . 'Commander': both famous calypso singer contemporaries of Spoiler; 'Attila the Hun' died in 1962, though he was considerably older than Spoiler, aged 70 by then.

'picong': dialect word for improvised, spontaneous verbal battle in rhymed song between two or more competing calypso singers.

p.436

'scrunter': dialect word for a down and out, victim of hard times.

'Arnold's Phoenician trader': protagonist in Edwin Lester Arnold's popular fantasy novel *Wonderful Adventures of Phra the Phoenician* (1890).

p. 437

'Tagore': the great Bengali poet, Nobel prize winning writer, and reformer, Rabindranath Tagore (1861–1941).

'bagasse': mass of dried pith left over from sugar canes, after the syrup has been extracted mechanically.

'hell . . . organize in soaring circles': a reference to the vision of hell in Dante's *Inferno*: a vast, conically shaped cavity, opening out below the surface of the earth, with its vortex at the earth's centre where a gigantic figure of Satan is embedded eternally in ice.

'the Duke of Iron': stage name for another calypso contemporary of Spoiler. But perhaps also invoking the 'Iron Duke', which was a nick-name given to the first Duke of Wellington, who was frequently a target of Byron's satirical jibes?

'contending for the monarchy': a reference to the 'calypso crown', but perhaps alluding also to Milton's Satan, who deems it 'better to reign in hell, than to serve in heaven'.

Chapter 6

Diaspora consciousness

Identity and exile in Caribbean British poetry

Morag Styles and Beverley Bryan

Introduction

For most Caribbean British poets, even those who were born in the UK, living in Britain involves compromise. Even though they can enjoy a rich cultural life with publishing and performance opportunities less available in the Caribbean, they also have to accommodate to a colonial past, a brutal history and racism. Most Caribbean/British poets also continue to have a strong relationship with their own particular place of origin, which often involves a complex mixture of emotions, including longing for home, ambiguous feelings about privilege and, for some, a sense of exile. While we might like to consider the Caribbean/British experience in a positive light—a sort of 'hybridity' that Marwan Kraidy ironically describes as the 'celebration of cultural difference and fusion' (2005: 1)—it may more aptly be seen as a pull in two opposing directions which has an intense effect on poets' sense of identity. Derek Walcott (2007) expresses power-fully such conflicting sentiments in this short extract from 'The Light of the World', where the poet who has moved away from his roots (St Lucia in this case) for 'better things' in the USA, returns to his native island, experiencing alienation, loss and profound sadness.

> Because I felt a great love that could bring me to tears,
> and pity that prickled my eyes like a nettle,
> I was afraid I might suddenly start sobbing
> on the public transport with the Marley going,
> and a small boy peering over the shoulders
> of the driver and me at the lights coming,
> at the rush of the road in the country darkness,
> and lamps in the houses on the small hills,
> and thickets of stars; I had abandoned them,
> I had left them on earth, I left them to sing
> Marley's songs of a sadness as real as the smell
> of rain on dry earth, or the smell of damp sand,
> and the bus felt warm with their neighbourliness,
> their consideration, and the polite partings.

Background

To understand Caribbean British poetry some background is necessary. Britain's selective immigration policy with regard to the Caribbean resulted in the uneasy settlement of Caribbean communities at the end of the Second World War. The turning point in this black diaspora was

1958 and the docking of the *Empire Windrush*. The migrants were mostly working class and poor, gravitating to places of work in London such as Brixton and Notting Hill, or Birmingham (Handsworth) or Manchester (Moss Side) or Leeds (Chapeltown). However, among these settlers, there were also students who came to take up scholarships at top universities.

Increasingly, the poor employment prospects in their home countries became a powerful push factor towards Caribbean migration to Britain. The pull factor was the fact that they were invited to fill positions English workers could or would not fill in the period of post-war reconstruction. Responses to the immigrants in Britain ranged from the barely curious, to the naively condescending but gradually became more hostile as West Indian workers increasingly availed themselves of the opportunities offered away from their homelands. Louise Bennett (1966) beautifully captures some of these tensions in her ironically amusing poem, 'Colonisation in Reverse'.

> . . .
>
> What an islan! What a people!
> Man an woman, old an young
> Jus a pack dem bag an baggage
> An turn history upside dung!
>
> Some people doan like travel,
> But fe show dem loyalty
> Dem all a open up cheap-fare-
> To-England agency.
>
> An week by week dem shipping off
> Dem countryman like fire,
> Fe immigrate an populate
> De seat a de Empire . . .

There were early problems for the settlers especially with finding accommodation from wary host communities but the migrants forced together by circumstances, pooled their own financial resources in 'pardner'[1] systems to secure places to live, often in crowded multi-occupier situations. Thus West Indian migrants found ways of making life possible and the number grew to nearly sixty thousand over a ten year period. However, these economic avenues closed abruptly with the Commonwealth Immigration Acts of the early 1960s—the first of several such attempts to limit Caribbean migration. This galvanised parents who had left their children in the Caribbean to seek the means to be re-united. It was the children of these immigrants who were part of the education system in the 1960s and 1970s—just as the UK was going through a process of comprehensive re-organisation, which was to have a significant impact on the whole system. The children would have come from the hills of Clarendon, the valleys of Portland, the backwaters of Port of Spain to cramped accommodation in the high-rise landscapes of Britain's inner cities. They experienced the hostility of an alien environment (McNeal and Rogers, 1971) and misrepresentation in the education system. The controversy of educationally subnormal (ESN) schools was a case in point. Some children arriving from the Caribbean with their varying Creoles and different discourse patterns were judged to be unfit for normal schools and parents, in ignorance, accepted the "specialness" of the schools they were invited to send their children to (Bryan et al., 1985). Edwards (1979) set up one of the early investigations into the 'language issue', to undo several misconceptions on such matters as the non-standard nature of Jamaican Creole and the related cognitive deficit of its speakers.

There was also hostility from the police, as these young West Indian migrants began to grow up in the UK's inner cities. One mechanism for these regular confrontations was the 'sus law', which gave the police powers to stop and search young people deemed suspicious. (We are ashamed to say that as we write this in 2013, there are news reports that the brother of the murdered schoolboy, Stephen Lawrence, has written to complain to the Police Commission about being stopped and searched for no good reason on numerous occasions.) James Berry's ironic 'In-a Brixton Markit' (1988) captures the outrage of young black men during the 1970s who were continually targeted by police while going about their lawful business:

And wha them si in deh?
Two piece a yam, a dasheen,
a han a banana, a piece of pork
an mi lates Bob Marley.

Their anger was compounded by the fact that the majority of them were British born rather than migrants. They saw the UK as their home and responded to legal questioning with native assertiveness. A number of community writing workshops and publishing cooperatives such as Black Ink helped to coordinate, fashion and express that sense of injustice through creative outlets.

At the same time, the middle-class migrants of the Caribbean who came as students interacted uneasily with the growing settler community. Their preoccupations were often with the emerging push toward self-governance and independence in their home countries in the Caribbean. In Jamaica, for example, the first Cabinet of 1957 included the first black Minister of Education. The migrant student population was in a hurry to return to the politics of de-colonisation, but whilst in the UK those so inclined formed the Caribbean Artists Movement (CAM), the 'back home' writers movement, as the outlet for their aesthetic endeavours. Fissures were soon revealed between the two communities of working-class settlers and the educated middle class.

In *Snow on Sugarcane: the Evolution of West Indian Poetry in Britain,* Dieffenthaller (2009) argues that the poet, Kamau Brathwaite, who was educated at Cambridge, straddled the divide between CAM's concern for poetic sensibility and the more prosaic concerns of the settlers who wanted to express the reality of living in Britain rather than a continuing hankering for 'home'.[2] These differences were exacerbated by increased racist attacks that culminated in the infamous 'rivers of blood' speech by Smethwick MP, Enoch Powell. For the settlers it was a period of organising into community groups, youth groups, Black Power organisations and Afro-centric groups—first against immigration laws and then against police harassment and discrimination, especially in education at the beginning, but later also about housing and health. By the mid 1970s, women were also setting up their own organisations to promote their specific concerns as well as Black community issues. National campaigns came after major atrocities such as the New Cross Fire of 1985 where thirteen young black people died under what was at the time seen as questionable circumstances.

At the same time, there was considerable cultural questioning in the evolving settler community—an illustration 'that identity is, first and foremost, socially constructed and therefore open to interrogation and redefinition' (Bryan, 1998). Initially, naming was a major issue—should it be West Indian, Caribbean, Black British, Afro-Caribbean or African-Caribbean?

There were also problematic assumptions and definitions about identity in the search for a sense of place:

> Home, my mother says, is in Jamaica but my father says that home is where we are now. My brother Carlton says home is in Africa. But he can't say if he means in the past or in the future. My sisters, they say they are English so that home is no problem for them. How can they all say these different things?
>
> (Garrison, 1979: 7).

A multiplicity of ethnicities is offered by Garrison's respondent family, underscoring the dominant relationship of young people with the host country as 'a fluctuating sense of belonging' (Bryan, 1998). The poetry of this period gives voice to these histories and struggles of the Black experience in Britain.

In some ways, the poets we consider in this chapter exemplify the tradition of Caribbean poetry in its political consciousness and its subversion of colonial cultural norms but, because of the intensity of the migration experience, the themes are at the same time visceral and affirming. They may deal with questions of identity and exile but they also find strategies of resistance through humour and a sly simplicity of rhyme and rhythm that engages and disarms. Through experience of loss, separation and hostility, the best of them use resistance to re-make something new—a new life and a new culture of resilience that relies on community resources. They were also willing to challenge existing orthodoxies: Caribbean British poets, for example, more than any other group, challenged the language of empire:

> I have crossed the ocean
> I have lost my tongue
> from the root of the old one
> A new one has sprung
> (Nichols, 1984: 64)

Indeed, some of these poets went even further and through their own process of creolisation created a new poetics, a sub-set of nation language that became world famous—dub poetry.

Caribbean British poetry really began to flourish in the late 1970s and early 1980s although Brathwaite, who was living in Britain at the time, had already published his influential *New World Trilogy* for OUP in 1973.[3] This was an exciting period for the development of Caribbean poetry with legendary performances taking place at Black Book Fairs in Brixton,[4] London, radical bookshops such as New Beacon Books and Bogle L'Ouverture Press promoting Caribbean writing, and talented poets such as John Agard, James Berry, Valerie Bloom, Grace Nichols and Benjamin Zephaniah beginning to publish for children as well as adults. This group was enthusiastically taken up by schools, libraries and festivals and began successful careers as writers and performers, all of them still popular today. Although each poet has a distinctive voice and style, there are common elements in their work. In this chapter, we draw on Caribbean British poetry for secondary students and adults, plus offering an occasional reference to poetry for a younger age group.

Back-home memories

In this section we touch on Caribbean poetry that focuses on the separation from home islands bringing with it potent memories, loss and readjustment. Indeed, Grace Nichols' first collection for children is titled, *Come on into my Tropical Garden* (1988) and it is full of references to Guyana.

> My imagination is stirred by my childhood. I was awakened by tropical things . . . whenever I remember the country village along the Guyana coast, where I spent my small-girl days, I can't help seeing water water everywhere. Brown silky water when it rained heavily. Fish swimming into people's yards and children catching them in old baskets . . . A lot of my poems are about . . . back-home happenings . . .
>
> (quoted in Styles and Cook, 1988: 7)

Nichols paints a picture of Guyanese life through honest and amusing portraits of people with lively incidents, local colour, animals and the natural world. 'Sea Timeless Song', for example, is much anthologised, popular for its haunting refrain ('sea timeless') and is perfect for choral speaking. In three couplet verses, Nichols mentions hurricanes, tourists and hibiscus that will 'bloom and dry wither so'. So what might pupils get out of this simple poem?

They can see/hear how the sound of the sea and the rhythm of the tide coming out and coming in *timelessly* is reflected in the metre. Like some Caribbean poetry, it is written in dactyls (one long stressed syllable, followed by two short unstressed syllables), rather than the iambic pentameter metre more common in English verse. Students can quickly note the repetition, alliteration and choice of soft sibilants in Nichols' poem. It is not exactly written in Standard English, nor does she use the basilectal Guyanese Creole of her home country. Nichols inserts some identifiable Creole markers such as 'Hurricane come' and this code-mixing gives it a distinctive Caribbean flavour.

The poem draws attention to the fact that the sea is always a constant in the Caribbean. Many islands are only a few miles wide and long so you never get away from the sea, which is a source of life, food and work. (Guyana is, of course, coastal rather than being an island.) But sun and sea comes at a price—hurricanes can bring devastating consequences to the islands with high human and economic costs. Extremes of weather also bring danger of environmental change including rising sea levels.

Visits to the Caribbean may be seen as exotic refreshment for tourists with its opportunities for sport, leisure and luxury, but that means 'service' for Caribbean people. So while tourism is an important industry for the Caribbean, the downside is the memory of a colonial past, the potential for spoiling the environment and the destructive effects of poverty living side by side with affluence. Olive Senior tackles this topic in a brilliant poem, 'Meditation on Yellow' in *Gardening in the Tropics* (2005). In his essay, 'Tourist, Traveller, Troublemaker' (2007), Stewart Brown draws on Jamaica Kinkaid to explore the range of attitudes adopted by those who visit these islands as strangers—made free to celebrate 'a self-deluded "freedom" in fantasy'.

The positioning of Caribbean islands means looking out to the Atlantic, Americas and Africa and all they configure, such as that horrific crossing-place of the past—the Middle Passage. If you do not look out to sea then you look inwards—and that can lead to tension between what home offers and its limitations. In the background of this short, apparently artless poem, lies the exploitation of the Caribbean by colonisers whom we could see as having turned over time into the more benign interlopers we call tourists. The poem, which can be appreciated by quite young children as well as adults, offers a gentle way into Caribbean poetry and its references to the beauty of Caribbean flora and fauna can be linked to issues of sustainability, the environment or simply the life cycle with its image of hibiscus blooming and withering.

Nichols has lived in Britain for most of her adult life and her poetry, for adults and children, often touches amusingly on the contrasts between life 'back home' and in England. However, the brutal legacies of Caribbean histories are never far away. Beneath the sensuality of another poem referring to 'Hibiscus' lie the painful lines 'red, open and not without sorrow/like your people'. 'Wherever I Hang', however, offers a different perspective on the diasporic condition, rather more playful and optimistic. It tells the story of feeling 'divided to de ocean/Divided to de bone', another hallmark of Caribbean poetry, beginning with longing for the 'warmth' and informality of Caribbean home life, contrasting it with the 'greyness', cold and conformity of life in Britain, which is affectionately mocked. 'To tell you de truth/I don't know really where I belaang', succinctly evokes the central trope of conflicted identity experienced by so many Caribbean writers. However, this ambiguity or 'double consciousness' can also carry a positive charge as in this poem, which ends on a triumphant note with 'Wherever I hang me knickers—that's my home.' This upbeat ending always makes the audience laugh; this brings us to the second feature of Caribbean British poetry we want to explore—humour. Many Caribbean poets write in an exuberant and witty fashion that readers and audiences adore but the laughter often has a serious, biting edge. This will be explored in the section below.

Humour that bites

The popular poet, Valerie Bloom, is an accomplished performer. She draws both on her Jamaican childhood and life in the UK in a lively Creole that is often likened to the work of Louise Bennett. Her collections usually contain a glossary of Jamaican Creole as Bloom is keen for her audiences to understand and appreciate her particular nation language when she gives readings.

Bloom is best known in the UK for her children's poetry, which exhibits a lightness of touch, a nice sense of fun, and makes many amusing references to her native Jamaica. However, when writing for an older audience, she can be more political. In *Touch Mi, Tell Mi* (1983), for example, in her short poem, 'Yuh Hear Bout?', she asks a series of ironic questions, such as 'you hear bout' policemen being held to account for beating up black 'bwoys without a cause'. Each answer ends with 'Me neidda'.

John Agard, originally from Guyana, has lived in the UK for many years. He is the 2012 winner of the Queen's Award for poetry, a distinction that probably occasions a mixture of pride and disbelief as his poetry, over forty years, has deftly and wittily challenged readers on issues of racism and injustice. As the writer and critic David Dabydeen aptly put it: 'John Agard's poetry is a wonderful affirmation of life, in a language that is as vital and joyous as we are able to craft it in the Caribbean, in spite of our history of distress' (www.poetryarchive. org/poetryarchive/singlePoem.do?poemId = 14751, online review, accessed 7 May 2013). Even in his first collection aimed at under sevens (*I Din Do Nuttin*, 1984), Agard gently opened up the delicate areas of identity, self-awareness and race in the otherwise bubbly 'Happy Birthday Dilroy'. He does so in a way that young readers can think about if they are alert to the issue, but ignore if they are not ready, as the child protagonist simply asks, 'Why the boy on the card so white?'

Agard has become one of the best loved poets in the UK. He has a sense of humour and warmth of personality combined with a biting satire that makes him a great favourite with children, adults and teachers alike. His range is impressive, recent output including two collaborations with illustrator Satoshi Kitamura—a version of Dante for teenagers (*The Young*

Inferno, 2008) and playful fables of our time (*Goldilocks on CCTV*, 2012), as well as themed collections on everything from maths to fairy tales, and edited anthologies on Caribbean poetry and the oral tradition (with Grace Nichols). It is worth pausing at the titles of recent collections for adults, which typify some of the points we are making in this chapter: *Travel Light, Travel Dark* (2013), *We Brits* (2007), note that Agard appears to be defining himself as a 'Brit', and his selected poems, *Alternative Anthem* (2009) is a good place for new readers to start, especially as it contains a DVD.

Particular poems by Agard have already gained classic status, some from his adult collections finding their way into examination syllabi. 'Poetry Jump-up', a celebration of carnival, has become a performance standard while the clever use of mockery in poems such as 'Half-Caste', 'Checking Out Me History' and 'Palm Tree King' are widely admired and can be found in *Get Back, Pimple!* (1996). 'English Girl Eats her First Mango' is full of sensuous language—'sundizzy/tonguelicking juicy/mouthwater flow/ripe with love/from the tropics'. As the poet shows the English girl how to 'lick', 'nibble', 'squeeze' and 'suck' the sweet fruit—a mixture of sexuality and politics—he makes an amusing intertextual reference to the Bennett poem, quoted above:

> man just lick
> your finger
> you call that
> culture
> lick your finger
> you call that
> culture
>
> unless you prefer
> to call it
> *colonization*
> *in reverse.*
>   (Agard, 2009: 21–3, our emphasis)

'Limbo Dancer at Immigration' is painfully amusing: painful because it alludes to some of the horrors of slavery; amusing because it pokes fun at racism in general and ignorant immigration officers in particular.

COUNTRY OF ORIGIN: SLAVESHIP
...
Suppose you got here on a banana boat
the authorities sniggered.

This is satire that stings. Cultural stereotypes are being ironically drawn into play and certain key phrases explode into new levels of significance.

ANY IDENTIFYING MARKS?
...
And when limbo dancer revealed ankles
bruised with the memory of chains
            it meant nothing to them

Although the language and ideas appear initially very accessible, the poem invites deeper engagement with ideas of identity and place, history and voice.

> So limbo dancer smiled
> saying I have nothing to declare
> & to the sound of drum disappeared.
>   (Agard, 1996: 48–9)

Maura Dooley writes of Agard's poetry as 'direct and arresting', 'full of startling imagery', 'passionate and erotic as often as they are political—often managing to be all these things at once' (http://www.bloodaxebooks.com/titlepage.asp?isbn=1852249919, online review, accessed 11 May 2013). She sums up in a nutshell why Agard's amusing, ironical yet urgent voice has created such a stir in the UK and has been taken to the hearts of so many readers.

Another Caribbean/British poet who has made a strong impact on British poetry is Benjamin Zephaniah. Like Agard, he is very funny, an electrifying performer, producing powerful effects on his audiences. His visually arresting collections are very popular with children and young adults alike. One thing that makes him special is that he was born in the UK yet he has chosen to explore his Jamaican identity prominently in his poetry, as well as to use the Jamaican language.

> I am de rapping rasta
> I rap de lyrics fasta
> Dan a Ford Cortina
> Or a double ghetto blasta . . .

Zephaniah's work offers a humorous but sharp critique of British society as a fully fledged member of that society. His 'Hip-Hop Cop', for example, is a lot of fun but look a bit more closely and Zephaniah also has something serious to say about policing in UK.

> When de hip-hop cop
> Is in fine style
> Michael Jackson
> Runs a mile
> An folk like me
> Shout hip-hooray,
> Why can't all coppers
> Dance dis way.
>   (Zephaniah, 1996b: 26)

Zephaniah's 'Reggae Head' is represented on the Poetry Archive and is suitable for secondary classrooms. Pupils can be encouraged to examine Zephaniah's use of music as a metaphor, while the language of oppression and resistance can also be traced throughout the poem. Readers may begin by noticing specific references to music (reggae, riddim, rock, pop, dub . . .) and go on to realise how a poem that seems quite light and positive at first quickly moves into more unsettling territory with a description of a Big-Brother-type society with its pills, police cells and psychiatrists, where ordinary people feel under siege from those who should be protecting them. Even worse, he points to racism by the state moving in a decisive way to corral the life chances of a particular segment of society.

A noticeable feature of Zephaniah's work is his choice of language that draws on his Jamaican heritage although he was born in England. Varieties of Jamaican Creole influenced the speech of children brought up in England who had adopted some forms and linguistic markers of their parents. Researchers have explored the language thus created through code-switching and the mixing of varieties on an individual basis, and suggested that it is first and foremost a cultural acquisition, a signalling system and a means of projecting identity. Zephaniah's poetry has a gentler side; he is as likely to be saying that 'There is good in everyone' (from 'Good Hope', 1996) and proclaiming a message of peace, love, veganism, concern for animals, as challenging the reader to confront racism. His poetry reaches out to young people who respond to both his sense of humour and to his humanity.

We have seen that Caribbean poetry, even that aimed at the young, is full of hope and optimism but has its sombre moments. The light reflects the vitality, versatility and variety of the writing; colourful references to the Caribbean and its sun, sea, characters, environment; the sheer fun and lightness of touch many poets exhibit; the rhythm and music of the poetry. The sombre moments make reference to the history of slavery, oppression and racism, which cannot be ignored. However, most poets writing for a younger readership lighten these themes by using irony and wit to make serious points.

'Mi own sense a time': the poetry of Linton Kwesi Johnson

When considering Caribbean/British poetry, the name of Linton Kwesi Johnson looms large, as it was Johnson who radically changed the tone and focus of language used by poets of Caribbean origin in the UK. Indeed, his poetry exhibits 'the tension between Jamaican Creole and Jamaican English and between those and English English' (Johnson, 1978: 8). Johnson was born in Chapelton, Jamaica, in 1952, leaving for Brixton, London, aged eleven, to join his mother who had emigrated earlier. Widely regarded as the greatest Caribbean British poet of his generation, Johnson pioneered a new kind of poetry using modified Jamaican English with a reggae rhythm, gaining a wide audience through his outstanding performances, musical brilliance and radical political message. Most of his work is recorded musically as well as in print and he would regard himself as much a musician as he is poet. Johnson's poetry often touches specifically on life in London as he gives voice against oppression. He is admired as a trusted recorder of social experience, attempting to 'express the anger and the frustrations and the hopes and the aspirations of my generation growing up in this country under the shadow of racism' (quoted in Dieffenthaller, 2009: 112). Johnson often refers back to his native Jamaica with criticism as well as affection. He became 'repelled by the narrowness of Jamaican society and the violence that permeated it—a revulsion that was unfortunately later confirmed by the murder by political thugs in Jamaica in 1983 of the poet Michael Smith, whose work Johnson had promoted' (Stewart, 1993: 81–2).

Johnson did not refer to himself initially as a dub poet and indeed tried to distance himself from the label, even though he was part of the delineation and definition of the term. In his discussion of the work of Michael Smith, Johnson admits that he first used the term 'dub lyricism' to describe the style of the reggae deejays evident in Jamaican rebel music at the time. He describes his own work as 'reggae poetry' to acknowledge the synthesis and linkages between the rhythmic lyrics of the creative voice and the lyrical rhythms of the reggae music evident in this genre and his own poetry. In reviewing the literature on dub poetry, Johnson settles on Mervyn Morris's definition as the poetic technique 'borrowed from recording technology where it refers to the activity of adding or removing sounds . . . written to be performed, incorporating a music beat, often a reggae beat. Often but not always the perfor- mance is done to the accompaniment of music recorded or live . . . written in the Jamaican language . . . [and] politically focused' (Johnson, 2007a: 155–6).

Some British readers find Johnson's powerful but idiosyncratic version of nation language challenging as he, like most Caribbean poets, followed an individual orthography or way of representing the language that we call 'eye Creole'. Caribbean linguists, in their attempt to promote and legitimate the vernaculars of the region, have supported the use of the Cassidy-Le Page phonemic script in a push for standardisation of these marginalised languages. However, use of this script has not been widespread. The idea of marginality and of even recovering voicelessness has been given a new disruptive interpretation by Brathwaite with his inimitable Sycorax Video Style using new fonts, typefaces and visual alignments to characterise the text of his later work (see *Barabajan Poems,* 1994, and *Born to Slow Horses,* 2005).

Johnson experimented for some time 'with diction, theme, and style, searching for his own voice' (Stewart, 1993). He found both inspiration and a resonance from his own immigrant experience, whose 'dominating themes [were] the tension between childhood memories of a colonial homeland and [the] mundane daily experience in an alien capital' (U Tam'si, 1972: xiii). Johnson went on to experiment with the:

> call and response or crier and chorus structure that was employed by Okigbo, who had adapted the method from the ancient oral tradition of African verse and story telling . . . also typical of Jamaican Rastafarian psalmody, and, indeed, of a long Afro- Jamaican tradition of worksongs and spirituals.
>
> (Stewart, 1993: 7)

Out of this energetic experimentation in the early 1970s came Johnson's first book, *Voices of the Living and the Dead* (1974), followed by *Dread, Beat an Blood* (1978), which includes the powerful poem, 'Five Nights of Bleeding', where 'the poet criti- cally comments on the activities of black youth . . . who direct their violence among themselves:

> **rebellion rushing down the wrong road,**
> **storm blowing down the wrong tree.**

Johnson 'conveys an ambivalence toward the music in which his rhythm is based. On the one hand, the dread throbbing of the dub-style reggae is not cathartic but compounds the inner rage of marginalised and alienated youth. On the other, the music is seen as an actual and metaphorical source of vindication and identity—renewing, enabling, and strengthen- ing, as in *Street* 66:

> **"outta dis rock**
> **shall come**
> **a greena riddim"'**
>   (Stewart, 1993: 77)

Inglan is a Bitch was published in 1980, the title indicating the content, followed by *Tings an' Times* (1991). Many of the best poems from all his collections can be consulted in Johnson's

Selected Poems, Mi Revalueshanary Fren (2002). Johnson's work is much admired. The distinguished poet, Fred D'Aguiar compares Johnson's poetry to traditional forms, writing that he 'maintains a reggae rhythm and a regular iambic mostly tetrameter line-beat . . . sustaining a rhyme-scheme locked to a few rhyming sounds, same word sounds or word endings, rather like a ballad, sestina or villanelle . . . with striking imagery and phrasing' (2002: xi). Kwame Dawes writes appreciatively of Johnson's ability to use a 'reggae aesthetic' with its 'rhythms, language and religious base in conjunction with Marxism and European politics' (in Dieffenthaller, 2009: 6).

One of Johnson's most moving poems is 'Reggae fi Dada'. It is a painful, compassionate poem where the poet's outrage about 'di anguish an di pain' suffered by his father who 'nevah ad noh life fi live' is tinged with resignation. The pain is not only in learning that his father has died as we follow the poet making the long sad journey to his graveside in Kingston, Jamaica—but in the recognition of the limitations Dada had suffered all his life—'wen mi reach mi sunny isle/ it woz di same ole style/di money well dry/di bullets dem a fly/ plenty innocents a die . . . ' The emotion of the situation is held in check, only just, as the poet remembers Dada 'strugglin in vain/fi mek two enz meet/soh dat dem pickney couda get/a likkle something fi eat/fi put cloaz pan dem back . . . ' The adult son's use of the childlike 'Dada' adds tenderness, encouraging empathy in the reader. The poet mourns the poverty and dead-end nature of Dada's life in a society of 'guarded affluence/di arrogant vices/cowl eyes of kantemp'. There are moments of sombre lyricism as 'di lan . . . sinkin in a sea of calamity/where fear breed shadows/dat lurks in di daak . . . '. Accentuated by imagery of a neglected landscape that is 'brown', 'soh many trees/cut doun/an di lan "owevahgrown"'. The poem ends on an informal local note, which adds poignancy by its very specificity—August Town cemetery where Dada will lie 'near to mhum an cousin Daris'. The power of this poem comes from its orality, the sound it makes as its reggae undertone emphasises regret and loss—the loss of a loved person and disillusionment about a society of violence and inequality that neglects what matters—its people and the environment they live in. Dada never stood a chance as 'di dice dem loaded/an di card pack fix'. It's not only Inglan that comes in for Johnson's excoriating cry for social justice. Here he expresses a love/hate relationship with Jamaica, a recoil from its inequality as he reflects on his father's life in a tender elegaic tone.

'If I Woz a Tap-Natch Poet'[5] is recorded on the Poetry Archive (and can be seen performed on YouTube). Johnson's use of the conditional—'if'—throughout the poem belies his message—that he, too, is 'tap-natch' and that soon 'goon poet haffi step in line' and recognise this fact. The first unattributed epigraph is taken from *The Oxford Companion to Twentieth-Century Poetry* (1994). In the entry on Linton K. Johnson, Mario Relich writes: 'the style of "dub poetry" has been described by James Berry as "over-compensation for deprivation"'. Johnson's poem is largely a response to that comment and the supposed author of it. The second epigraph begins the counterattack. 'If I Woz a Tap-Natch Poet' praises all the poets it names. The poem associates the persona with Mandela (a political progressive) and the unnamed poet with Buthelezi.[6] There may also be a degree of self-referential enjoyment by Johnson, 'sending up' his own place in the canon. In the poem, he refers to groups of poets, beginning with those, including Walcott, who have followed 'Western' poetic models. He moves to consider poets regarded as more 'rooted' in Caribbean folklore and history, such as Kamau Brathwaite, and finishes with a group who can write 'a poem/soh beautiful dat it simple'. He praises all these poets in figurative language—Walcott's poetry is 'like a precious/memari/whe make yu weep' and Brathwaite's like 'a ole time calypso ar a slave song/dat get ban'. Yet he needs reach for no metaphors asserting his own poetic identity:

> still
> inna di meantime
> wid mi riddim
> wid mi rime
> wid mi ruff base line
> wid mi own sense a time

By the end, his apparent self-deprecation is a deliberate false modesty, as he criticises some of the other poets with their 'vaig fleetin hint af hawtenticity'.

In an article in *Textual Practice,* Robert McGill (2003) suggests that Johnson himself may be 'stepping in line' by using the sort of discourse associated with 'tap-natch poets' and entering the canon of Penguin classics with its scholarly introductions, footnotes and cover blurbs 'that assert literary merit'. McGill goes on to argue that the somewhat perplexing references to Mandela and 'Bootahlazy' make it essentially a political poem, pointing out that the poem was first performed when South African politics were high profile internationally and where the number of supporters for both candidates in the 1994 election was crucial—'touzans a touzans a touzans'. McGill also wonders whether Johnson was getting in a sly dig, comparing Walcott's 'individualistic' 1992 Nobel Prize for Literature with Mandela's 1993 Nobel Peace Prize and 'its call for unity among peoples'. Or even, perhaps, a dig at himself positioned somewhere between 'musician and poet, between high art and popular culture, between politics and aesthetics'.

The poem certainly has a Calypsonian 'flourish' as Johnson both mocks himself *and* simultaneously asserts his own place in the Western literary canon—and it's his use of 'riddim' and musical language that marks his claim to 'authenticity'. Together with his defiant use of non-standard spelling and grammar—his own 'eye Creole'—he is making a 'political' point about the need for a new poetic language in which to express a confident, post-colonial identity.

The future of Caribbean British poetry

We have mainly concentrated on well-established Caribbean British poets of an older generation in this chapter. We regret that space does not allow a great many fine Caribbean British poets to be discussed and we would recommend readers who want to extend their knowledge of this poetry to consult anthologies such as *Red: Contemporary Black British Poetry* (2010), edited by Kwame Dawes.

However, we are happy to conclude by pointing out that there is a supremely talented younger generation of poets with distinctive voices making a strong impression in the UK and internationally. Of the many possibilities, we have selected two 'second generation' poets who have worked on the project with us—Dorothea Smartt and Anthony Joseph, respectively of Bajan and Trinidadian heritage. Interestingly, both of them, like many young Caribbean British poets today, work across the arts. In Smartt's case, she is co-director of Inscribe, the writer development programme of the excellent publishing house, Peepal Tree Press, as well as editor of a poetry magazine and a live artist who performs regularly in schools. Joseph is also a musician and novelist who tours with The Spasm Band and teaches creative writing at two London universities, Birkbeck College and Goldsmiths.

Acclaimed by Brathwaite, described by Blake Morrison as an 'exceptional talent', Joseph's poetry breaks new ground in his 'innovative blend of genres and styles [. . .] while experimental traditions enable him to show the diaspora in a fresh light' (http://eventful.com/performers/anthony-joseph-/P0–001–000267966–3, online review, accessed 11 May 2013). His themes find connection with other Caribbean British poets discussed so far, for example in his inclination towards autobiographical poetry of childhood memories of Trinidad and his exploration of exile, identity and ancestry, as exemplified in the extracts below from his first major volume, *Bird Head Son* (2009).

> Maman.
> Tell me again why I should leave this island.
> Tell me again that those cities exist.
> All I know of the ocean
> Is that a river
> starts here.[7]

> All these hills are home. All these cliffs and holy
> mountainsides.
> Holding on to my people and my people holding onto me and
> sudden so the rain came brewing down hard on the hills of mists
> of ghosts across the hillsides coming down on these shacks on
> these hills . . .[8]

Another distinctive feature of Joseph's poetry is the musicality of his voice which Christian Campbell describes as obsessed with 'performance, ritual and chant', while Earl Lovelace notes 'a music brimming with jazz energy [. . .] and calypso musings' (Lovelace, online review). *Rubber Orchestras* (2011) explodes on the page with 'Jelly Roll Morton /at the Cadillac café', gypsy music, jam sessions, jazz muggles, drummers, blues and riffs:

> . . . Burning in the night.
> In the ecstatic night,
> singing freedom songs
> at the church of electric sky music.[9]

The poet wends his way across 'dirty cities of the Mediterranean', 'Orinoco's fresh water streams', 'the hills of Montserrat', Haiti's 'heartland of rainforests', 'electric theatres/with guitars from Brazil' and the 'vibrant stars' of the Bahamas, as he touches down in Mali, the Congo, Egypt, North and South America, the Caribbean and, most tellingly, the 'vocal music of black Africa':

> where the slit-drum speaks its prayer of timbres
> each echo is a receptacle of traditional sounds,
> earth-bow, calabash, crocodile,
> stone.

Whereas Joseph mostly finds inspiration outside the UK, Dorothea Smartt is a 'Brit born Bajan' who writes about growing up in South London, about her parents and their heritage, as well as topics likely to interest young adults, such as shopping, hair, food and girlhood. Even so, 'back home' colours her poetry, demonstrating a strong allegiance to the Caribbean, Barbados in particular. She writes in a range of styles but a Bajan voice often comes through—not always a true Creole, but with markers that represent the folk, rather like Brathwaite himself. For example, 'Eclipse over Barbados' begins

> Look up man! Wha wrong wid d'moon?
> D'sky clear-clear, an' a t'ousand stars flickering,
> begging me look up. Dey are endless!
> (Smartt, 2008: 33–4)

Connecting Medium (2001) includes a powerful sequence of Black Medusa poems:

> ... believe it!
> she could turn a man t'stone
> some whiteman
> nightmare riding
> he mind across the centuries
> in turn turning we mad[10]

Smartt's poetry strongly foregrounds issues of gender, identity and exile. She makes reference to the sacrifices made by people of Caribbean origin working hard in the UK, only too aware that 'Back home's/always in mind.' There's the woman in Milton Keynes sending home end-of-line 'River Isand' clothing, 'stories of her whole village dressed bring a smile'. Or how:

> A text message beeps,
> riding the packed bus from work:
> 'wen can u sen £'.
> (2008)

Ship Shape (2008) includes a potent series of poems commissioned for a memorial to Lancaster's involvement in the slave trade. Borrowing Bob Dylan's words for a poem title, 'Bringing It All Back Home', Smartt reminds the reader of the dirty commercial aspect of slavery and the hypocrisy of those who 'enjoyed the benefits'.

> *Grocer?* You were a Slave trader!
> And everything has its price,
>
> and denial is only debt
> with interest to be paid.

More than half of this collection is made up of a series of poems based on the discovery of the grave of a slave, nicknamed 'Samboo'. One poem lists 99 names, many of them hostile, ugly and ignorant, used against black people. The simplicity of putting each name in a separate line gives a powerful indictment of racism though the poem begins and ends with love.

Bilal

beloved
son
brother
husband

. . .

heathen
cannibal
beast
blackamoor
darkie
nigger
uncivilised
wog

. . .

progeny
family
Bilal

Smartt's poetry has gleaned praise from a wide range of critics. Her work, featured on the Poetry Archive (2012), is described as crossing 'cultural boundaries with confident ease, speaking in the appropriate register, polishing diction with her eye and ear alive to its linguistic, musical and moral currency'.

Dorothea Smartt, Anthony Joseph and all the poets mentioned in this chapter could be described as chorus members of that 'vocal Caribbean Diaspora, laying claim to more distant, shared identities, which speak in different voices and draw on historic memory and myth'.[11] Whether these poets were born in UK or moved there later, and whatever they feel about the country where they live, diasporic consciousness pervades and enriches their work. Readers need to understand the urgency of this relationship in appreciating Caribbean British poetry.

Notes

1 'Pardner' is the Jamaican name for an informal co-operative saving system, used widely in many parts of the Caribbean and the diaspora (Senior, 2003: 375).
2 Brathwaite's seminal work is discussed in detail in Chapter 2.
3 *The Arrivants* is a composite of three individual collections—*Rights of Passage, Masks* and *Islands,* the first of which was published in 1967.
4 'Creation for Liberation' was the slogan for the book fairs. It emphasised that the writers were using their work as part of the movement for liberation. Later other artists used the name.
5 Discussion of this poem draws on work by Tessa Ware, Head of English, Alexandra Park School. Tessa has been closely involved with the CPP project since its inception. Her account of using Johnson's poetry with a class of twelve year olds is discussed in more detail in Chapter 9.
6 A footnote says: 'Chief Buthelezi, Chief of the Zulus during the anti-apartheid struggle in South Africa, militantly opposed to African National Congress that was led by Nelson Mandela.' We are grateful to Mervyn Morris for pointing out this fact and the sources of Johnson's poem.
7 From 'Bosch's Vision', *Bird Head Son* (2009).
8 From 'The Barber' (ibid.).
9 From 'Electric Sky Music', *Rubber Orchestras* (2011).
10 From 'Medusa: cuts both ways' (2009).
11 This quotation is taken from the Poetry Achive entry for Dorothea Smartt.

Chapter 7

Creating homeland

An introduction to contemporary Caribbean poetry

Lorna Down

In this chapter we consider several poems representative of the breadth of style and vision of contemporary Caribbean poetry, beginning with a few established poets and classic poems—Lorna Goodison's 'Mother the Great Stones Got to Move', Olive Senior's 'Meditation on Yellow', Dennis Scott's 'Guard ring', Merle Collins' 'Pearls', Eddie Baugh's 'Nigger Sweat' and Mervyn Morris' 'Muntu'. Complementing this work is that of a younger generation of outstanding poets: Christian Campbell, Kei Miller and Tanya Shirley, representing the broad range of fine post-Independence voices. Like many of the earlier poems, these are characterised by a rich infusion of traditional beliefs, engagement with the history of the region and rich depictions of the landscape. They are, however, distinguished by a greater variety in the forms used, more creative play with Caribbean languages as well as discovering and co-creating a present Caribbean homeland and its future. This chapter will focus on the latter.

Lorna Goodison: 'Mother the Great Stones Got to Move'

J. Edward Chamberlin (1993: 28) makes the point that for many West Indians loss and dispossession have been transformed into migration and exile and a quest for home. Goodison's poem, like the others in the chapter, may be seen as a response to that quest as it both signifies and creates place—a homeland—often shrouded by its history of loss. In the first stanza, the poet declares:

> In this hole is our side of the story . . .
> It is the half that has never been told, some of us
> must tell it.

A post-colonial reading of the history asserts the perspective of the formerly colonised. Yet even as the poet provides that perspective, uncovering a history of dispossession and a people reduced to 'exact figures/headcounts, burial artifacts . . . ', the poem insists on paying attention to what is here and now. That too is the narrative that needs to be told. Acknowledgement of that history, however, clears the way/removes one of the stones so that the Caribbean present 'home' and its continuing construction are revealed. It is against this backdrop that that poet's employment of the Revival song has to be heard:

> Mother the great stones got to move
> Mother, the great stones got to move

> Mother, the great stones got to move
> The stones of Babylon
> Mother, the great stones got to move

In referencing the Revival song, in using it as the title of the poem and a refrain throughout the poem, Goodison highlights the religious traditions of the 'ordinary' people. Revivalism is after all a Creole religious form—emerging from the Baptist churches yet distinguished by its African retentions (ACIJ, 2013). Significantly, the 'Mother' is the spiritual head of the revival church, the possessor of knowledge, of ancestral links and memory, a figure of power and authority. More often than not she is a working-class female by day but at night she becomes the chosen messenger, who 'catches' the spirit and becomes that link between the congregation and the ancestral spirits (Baker, 2004). Goodison then evokes not only the power of the 'Mother' but also the power of the 'ordinary' Caribbean people. As in Earl Lovelace's 'Wine of Astonishment' the folk religion symbolically represents the inherent power of a people to shape their own place as well as resist oppression and domination. And though they may be seen as 'small dreamers', like only 'small islanders', the poem re-presents them as the figure of the Mother is invested with deity-like status and the poem itself becomes a kind of prayer addressed to her:

> Mother, there is the stone on the hearts of some women and men
> . . . Speaking for the small
> dreamers of this earth, plagued with nightmares, yearning
> for healing dreams
> we want that stone to move

Moreover, the drumbeat of the Revival song, felt and heard in the rhythm of the poem, makes this invocation reverberate throughout. Most important, the refrain increasing in its intensity also points to a place where the 'small dreamers' have power, have voice and are visible. Home is thus constructed. So despite a history of power inequities, which persist into the present, as the poet's juxtaposition of past and present scenes of exploitation and dispossession makes transparent, the poem uncovers a place that is being created upon the traditions and beliefs of a people.

Ironically, what also gives shape and credibility to this place is the sense of the future. The drum's insistent beat, accompanying a Revival song that marks the passing of the old and an advent of the new, directs our attention to the future, to a time beyond that of a history of oppression. The poet links images of nursing mothers to the moon, to suggest the possibility for a new beginning, a nurturing place, a 'home' capable of taking the next generation to the desired future.

Shifting perspective from the localised scene to that of the universal and timeless, Goodison invokes the spiritual ancestors: 'Mother, the great stones over mankind got to move.'

What Goodison has achieved here is the creation of a spiritual homeland—a secure path to:

> . . . mount morning
> site of the rose quartz fountain
> brimming anise and star water
> bright fragrant for our children's future.

Olive Senior: 'Meditation on Yellow'

Olive Senior describes the writer as an interpreter, an artist who takes the 'journey beyond everyday reality, to stand at the "still point of the turning of the world", to look, listen, learn, and find our way back with something to say about the experience that will strike a chord for the reader, viewer or listener' (Morris and Allen, 2007: 159). In her poem 'Meditation on Yellow', Senior journeys beyond the present day reality to the past and returns to present her readers with the Caribbean landscape and its people re-constructed in their own and not the coloniser's images. Home is thus constructed from these 'revised readings' of the region's history.

In this poem, Senior's presentation of the landscape is one of bounty and fruitfulness, though never free of the scarring made by the history, politics and the socio-economics of place. Fixed formulations of identities are challenged and reconstituted, which leads to a recovery of self from a colonial discourse of exploitation and erasure. Divided into two parts, the poem focuses in part one on the first inhabitants in Jamaica, the Tainos, as well as the landscape.

Often presented as child-like in colonial discourse, the Tainos are re-imaged here. Asserting their difference to the colonisers, the persona declares:

> I like to feel alive
> to the possibilities
> of yellow

'Yellow' is of course a metaphor for the tropics, its sunlight, its warmth. Here the poet celebrates a people in touch with their land and with what is presented as 'the real wealth' of the natural landscape in contrast to the invaders' gold quest and gold lust:

> But it was gold
> on your mind
> gold the light
> in your eyes

The poet, moreover, shatters the image of the simple 'native'. The poem ironically opening with an apparent quiet, gentle, almost matter-of fact tone alludes to and subverts that image:

> At three in the afternoon
> you landed here at El Dorado

But this shifts dramatically as the El Dorado image is linked to the bracketed: '(for heat engenders gold and/fires the brain)' and the first stanza ends with a mocking tone:

> Had I known I would have
> brewed you up some yellow fever-grass
> and arsenic

By coupling these two images: fever grass known for its curative measures and arsenic, a metallic poisonous element, Senior introduces a contrast/a series of binaries that she employs to revise the image of colonised and coloniser. In tones that are in turn humorous, sarcastic and ironic the persona imagines an alternative history, one in which the peaceful Indians had recognised the violence and greed of the colonisers hidden in a show of gifts: 'a string of beads/and some hawk's bells'. What also emerges in this representation of the history, as Baker (2005) posited, is the Tainos' civilisation with its own ordered and unique way of life. A post-colonial perspective reveals a world disrupted and almost destroyed by Columbus' alleged civilising mission. The seemingly epic tale of his encounter with the Tainos is reduced to an invader's betrayal of trust, a craving for cold metals and an incapacity to recognise civility and hospitality.

In part two, there is a change in the landscape and 'home' emerges constructed in the limited spaces that a tourist economy allows. (Ironically, it is an economy that is the supposed bedrock of many of the islands in the Caribbean.) On one hand, there is the bounty of the landscape, on the other, is a continuing exploitation of the people. Framed as an address to the new colonial presence by one of the locals, the poet lists the various areas in which the exploitation has continued over different periods of the region's history. Reading like an inverted litany:

> I've been slaving in the cane rows
> for your sugar
> I've been ripening coffee beans
> for your morning break
> I've been dallying on the docks
> loading your bananas . . .

the stanza reveals a landscape whose riches are being 'mined' for others. The juxtaposition of images of enforced hard labour with images of cane rows, coffee beans, bananas, orange groves, ginger, cocoa pods and aluminium makes this clear. The landscape is now the province of the new arrivals. And though it is in a later poem, 'Reject Text for a Tourist Brochure', that the poet uncovers the ironic danger posed by a tourist economy, here she employs the landscape to reveal a strong resistance to this new form of exploitation—one not readily recognised.

What is clear is that one's place has to be claimed, has to be staked out. The awareness of possibilities of loss, of 'home' being destroyed, makes the need for such claiming even stronger, thus the protest:

> . . .
> And I reach to the stage where
> (though I not impolite)
> I have to say: lump it
> or leave it
> I can't give anymore

And the landscape is imaged as a part of this protest. So the trees and flowers: the allamanda, the cassia, the poui, the golden shower are 'street gals' and 'streggehs'—too wild to be contained. Their insistence on being, on 'flaunting themselves everywhere', reflects a people's possession of their place. They are no longer the patient, friendly Indians or the displaced African slaves but the descendants who are now ready to reclaim their land and build their home.

Senior's poem is, in effect, an acknowledgement of Caribbean place and, like Goodison she uncovers the fundamental power of the Caribbean people: their spiritual birthright and inner force to possess it: 'you cannot tear my song/from my throat/you cannot erase the memory/of my story/you cannot catch/my rhythm'. The poet in this list of affirmations declares that 'being' cannot be destroyed, that a people's spirit and soul are indefatigable— even as this declaration is qualified by the rider 'I want to feel' making it read like a prayer, a plea for salvation. Moreover, the final line 'any day now' in the last stanza, 'You cannot reverse/Bob Marley wailing/making me feel/so mellow/in that Caribbean yellow/at three o'clock/any day now', suggests a threat as well as a promise and a hope. The insistent though subtle sounds of resistance effected by the interplay of assonance and end-rhymes underline the changed persona—one who now recognises the invader in her Garden of Eden.

What Senior has done in this first poem in her collection, *Gardening in the Tropics*, is to show how socio-economic, historical and political realities are embedded in landscape. And yet despite the harshness of those realities, the imaginary recreation of a bountiful landscape filled with possibilities can map the contours of home.

Dennis Scott: 'Guard-ring'

> I going alone to mi house
> Wid the ring pon mi finger

To recognise and acknowledge a distinct Caribbean place is impelling for many in this region given its history of dispossession and homelessness. The first two poets not only do this but also engage in shaping this place. The Caribbean, at the intersection of so many different cultures and at the crossroads of different imperial powers, could easily have been assimilated. Guarding against such a possibility is the fact of creolisation—which Scott's poem 'Guard-ring' marks as the distinct shape of the Caribbean. Kamau Brathwaite (1975) has explained that creolisation may be seen as a fluidity of movement between races, cultural syncretism and a strong consciousness of an ancestral heartland, mainly African, Asian and Amerindian, however much the European forms have dominated the surface reality. He speaks of it as plurality and process, 'of multiform orientation from or "to-wards" ancestral origins' (1975: 7). Scott's poem enacts this creolisation, this mixing and blending of cultures through representing as 'natural' and 'normal' the fusion of the formal, established religion of Christianity, introduced by the Europeans, with that of an African-derived folk religion.

In effect, Scott may be seen as detailing the genesis of a distinct Caribbean tradition. As discussed earlier, the traditions are the foundation of a clearly defined Caribbean place. More so, Scott's poem expresses the desire for that safe place denoted 'home'.

This desire for home is expressed in a woman's desperate prayer for a safe arrival home. It is a prayer grounded in both the dominant Christian religion as well as the folk tradition. There is no irony here. There is also the poem's rhythm, which evokes the pocomania dance of the folk religion. The Church's disapproval for the folk religion is acknowledged and dismissed by the woman as she moves seamlessly between her address to the Lord and the practice of the folk religion, metonymically represented in the use of the rings:

> Watch where I walking, Lord
> Make mi foot step hard
> on the enemy's shadow
> an hear me.
>   I wearing de ring dem tonight-

The urgency of her situation demands a plural not a unitary approach. The image with which the poem opens 'Moon shadow burning . . . ' alludes to the many myths surrounding the moon that hint at mystifying danger. The images 'moon shadow falling', 'moonshine wetting mi face up', forms a backdrop to the persona's plea. In fact as the speaker lists all that she needs help with it becomes clear that it is help for all the mysterious calamities faced on life's journey—hate, malice, temptation, self-love, famine, drowning, fire, desire that threatens— 'de barracuta teet of desire'. It is all of these calamities that make the journey hazardous and life-threatening:

> I fraid for de shape of de winding –
> De road too crooked,
> It making a rope to twine me!

But the goal is clear; the persona is focused on the homestretch. There is also the recognition that to arrive home is not happenstance. It too is a learned process and as the persona draws on the two traditions the reader learns that both are necessary in order to complete the home journey. Scott's effortless code-switching and the fluid movement along the language continuum affirm this cultural blending. In fact, the poet cleverly interchanges the diction from one tradition with the other to show how 'naturally' they blend with each other:

> guard me asleep and awake!
> De ring did bless in de balm yard
> but Thee I praise.

There is also the serious and heightened use of the Creole to reveal the depth of the persona's plea. It is the heart language that is needed to convey the persona's powerful feelings and reflects strongly that consciousness of an ancestral heartland to which Brathwaite refers. The simplicity and earnestness of the prayer is thus accentuated. The short lines and the sounds of the Creole, for example the use of the 'd' of the Creole instead of 'the' of standard English, is employed as well to produce the incantatory effect of a prayer.

The fusing and the complementing of elements from both traditions continue throughout the poem (some not too dissimilar from each other) to reveal the process of creolisation. Slowly emerging is how creolisation 'roots' a people in their own landscape and how it empowers them. In 'Mother the Great Stones Got to Move', we see the creation of a spiritual homeland; here we explore the source of power there. Significantly, the poem ends with 'amen', an affirmation of this creolisation, an acceptance that this is as it is.

Scott's representation of this Creole space highlights a distinct feature of Caribbean life. The persona's journey home metaphorically represents that of the Caribbean's people. And arrival is shown as dependent on a recognition and an acknowledgement of that homeland's peculiar traditions. Scott's declaration in an earlier poem 'Homecoming' (Scott, 1973: 7) echoes this note of acceptance of one's cultural space:

> It is time to plant
> feet in our earth. The heart's metronome
> insists on this arc of islands
> as home.

Mervyn Morris: 'Muntu'

Given a history in which home and self have been devalued, Mervyn Morris's 'Muntu' is important for its quiet acceptance of home and its history. Like the other poets in this chapter, Morris acknowledges a homeland built on *iron clinks*. He recognises too the ancestors who remain 'alive inside the daylight', who cannot be erased, or contained in any discourse and any single lineage.

The title of the poem is aptly linked to Janheinz Jahn's book of the same name. It is a text that speaks to whether African culture has been assimilated into Western culture and so destroyed. In referencing that text and dedicating the poem to Jahn, Morris alludes to a distinctive Caribbean culture which has escaped total absorption.

The poet in his characteristic spare and minimalist style re-constructs the history of the region as he produces a genealogy of formidable fathers:

> Enter my father, laughing,
> a substantial black.
> . . .
>
> Behind him his black father,
> formidable, stern.

Morris draws our attention to their blackness, a distinguishing feature. Yet the father's entry marked with laughter invites us, however, to treat this 'lightly', to see the humour in the reference to 'a substantial black' and to the history that is often presented in sombre tones.

It is with that blend of seriousness and humour that Morris points out the incompleteness of the genealogy that he has just produced. There is the other side—'My mother's mother shuffles in/dragging her gentleness along the glare/She indicates her father/who looks white.' The allusion to the common representation of the 'civilising' European is clear. Morris plays on this depiction, inverting the binary descriptions of Africa and Europe—shuffling grandmothers contrasted with substantial fathers. At the same time he pokes gentle fun as he images that 'civilised' culture in terms of 'shuffles' and 'dragging'.

Morris also cleverly represents the grandmother's father as one 'who looks white' to suggest the creolisation that occurred. And by extension the 'substantial black' father cannot claim any purity of lineage. Moreover, there is just a casual nod of inclusion by the grandmother: 'She indicates her father.' Thus the dual heritage though acknowledged is lightly played; the mock-serious tone of the final lines ensures this: 'I start to hear the irons clink/He dissipates my terror with a wink.' The rhyming 'clink/wink' intimates an irreverent attitude towards this history of horror. Yet that clearly is not the case. What we have instead is an emotionally charged couplet that summarises the history of the region but which asks that we do not take ourselves too seriously.

Reading this poem in relation to another by Morris, 'Sentences for Heritage Week', makes clear the poet's point that history should not weigh heavily on one, that history should not be a 'sentence', a judgement. History instead should free one. So the poet's pun on 'sentences' reminds us of the art's possibilities for doing so. He tells us:

> Mine history
> for the energy it frees.

Morris' poem combines irony with humour. Showing the funny side to the most despairing of situations, the poet asks his readers to simply accept what is past and who we were and are. In doing so, we construct the home that is needed. Like Scott, Morris helps a people to see and to accept this Caribbean homeland filled with the surprises any excavation of its history may throw up.

Merle Collins: 'Pearls'

Questions of power, of hegemony often dominate colonial or post-colonial discourse; it is implicit in Scott's 'Guard-ring', for example. Creolisation subverts 'naturally' the power of the apparent dominant form. Merle Collins explores those questions as she examines a country's struggle for independence and non-alignment with powerful industrial nations. In doing so, she clarifies for us the political struggle for 'home'.

Independence from colonial powers marked a major step in the development of many of these countries but such independence did not mean a freedom from colonial or neo-colonial powers. During the 1960s and 1970s a number of these small island states attempted to chart their own course without being aligned to any superpower—as in Jamaica's Michael Manley-led non-aligned movement. 'Pearls' reminds us of that attempt to chart an independent course and to choose one's alignment. This attempt along with internal conflicts and politics ended in the Grenada invasion. 'Pearls' is one of three poems in Collins' collection *Lady in a Boat* (2003) that specifically addresses the politics of the islands.

The tongue-in-cheek comment by the persona: 'This experience is/precious' sets the tone as the poet uncovers layer by layer the ironies in the Grenada invasion. Focusing on a seemingly insignificant aspect—the search of a local's car for Cubans by United States marines—the poet gives us an intimate and personal rendering of the invasion and by extension the political situation in the region.

> When the marines stopped the car
> And ordered them out, he laughed.

The power of the 'other' has to be acknowledged and yet that power can be resisted. The persona laughs. It is a laugh that threads the poem and it is suggested that its form changes and intensifies. So his laugh is not only a sign of his powerlessness but also his resistance. His laughter is used as a weapon to protect him from the assault on his person. The laugh also exposes the action of the marines as folly and in doing so the image of the powerful is challenged:

> One marine said they
> were looking for Cubans, and
>
> he laughed. The marines lifted
> the mats off the floor of the
> car, and he laughed.

It is remarkable that the marines are not identified by country, but the simple unqualified word 'marines' set against the historical facts metonymically suggests the power and reach of the industrial north; and by an implied contrast the limitations of independence, of power for small island states.

The poet, however, suggests that the marginalised also contribute to their position of marginality. The persona's statement, '[this] is my country and/a foreign soldier just searched me' placed alongside '[but] we paid cash for it . . . we invited this' mark the complicity of the supposedly powerless in their subordination. The relationship between both groups is complex. The people forced to invite in the marines never bargained for their open establishment of authority, for their being 'inside/of your house and . . . acting/like it's theirs'.

Inherent in hegemonic relations is the matter of ownership; those in central places see marginal places as also belonging to them. But the poem challenges this. The persona's wry comment, 'I guess resisting would be/illegal' in recalling a similar historical instance 'Once, resisting slavery/was illegal' contests the idea of one being owned by another. The adverb placed significantly at the beginning of the line suggests both the possibility—it happened some time ago—but also the challenge. Slavery was after all resisted and effectively so in the many slave rebellions and also finally abolished. Moreover, the poem shows that resistance is an inherent part of hegemonic relations.

The last two stanzas are critical. They reveal two different reactions to this power play. The action of the woman, 'She watched/the road as she drove' suggests a new carefulness, an alertness to the path, to the future even as one continues on the way. In contrast, the man's laughter, 'he/laughed like he would never stop' opens up to multiple readings—a craziness, a deep sorrow, an anger.

Read in relation to 'Meditation on Yellow', 'Pearls' suggests a closure of hope. The spirit of defiance articulated in Senior's poem appears to have been broken. The image of protest in that poem as in 'you cannot tear my song/from my throat', is in direct opposition to the image of the silenced woman companion with which 'Pearls' ends:

> She glanced at
> him and was silent. She watched
> the road as she drove . . .

The poem raises the questions of how to protect home and whether small nation states can maintain independence. Such questions are partially answered as the distinction between 'belongers' and foreigners is insisted upon throughout the poem:

>   He
> said, The point is, they're inside
> of your house and they're acting
> like it's theirs.

What is clear is that any claim to place has to be staked and re-staked. Boundary lines marking home can easily be crossed especially if power relations are unequal.

Edward Baugh: 'Nigger Sweat'

The Caribbean is both a place of bounty and of want. The harsh social economic realities make northern cities, constructed as places of opportunity and of wealth, the goal of many Caribbean people. In his poem, 'Nigger Sweat', Edward Baugh explores this drive to migrate in a light, humorous, ironic yet very serious way. The title itself is ironic—with its allusion to a history in which 'nigger' was the contemptuous term used to belittle the black man; and his sweat was occasioned by that of the hard labour in the cane fields.

The immediate setting is, however, that of a familiar contemporary scene—the would-be migrant's encounter with the officer at the US embassy. Perhaps nowhere else is the power differential between people from the 'developing' world and those from the industrialised world more poignantly reflected than in the visa section of the foreign power on one's home ground. Here the display of power can make nationals feel small on their own soil. The sign in the waiting room of the US embassy reads 'Please have your passport and all documents out and ready for your interview. Kindly keep them dry.' Given the anxiety of these applicants who are often kept waiting in long lines in the sun to see the immigration officer, it would not be uncommon for them to have sweaty palms and wet documents.

The poem is an imaginary address to the immigration officer by a would-be migrant. His address is marked by an apparent respect and honesty, even a seeming subservience, as 'boss' suggests. However, throughout the poem the sub-text counters that—revealing a fine con-artist at work. The facade of the simple man masks that of the artist at work:

> No disrespect, mi boss
> just honest nigger sweat:
> well almost, for is true
> some of us trying to fool you . . .

He partially admits his 'anancyism' by pointing to the practice of others and he tries to explain the reason for the drive to get a visa at any cost:

> But, boss, is hard times
> make it, and not because
> black people born wutliss:
> so boss, excuse this nigger sweat

The poet is, however, also at work—recalling a history of oppression and exploitation, when the 'black man's sweat' was used to 'put the aroma/in your choice Virginia . . . '. He imagines also how such a history could conjure pictures of the officer, 'choking and drowning/in a sea of black man sweat' even as he urges that such feelings should be contained.

Juxtaposing the past oppression with that of the present, the poet suggests that little has changed. The persona recognises that the 'cool-cut, crew-cut Marine boy' does not recognise nor respect him. To the marine, he invisible. But the persona has the last laugh; he is aware of the Marine boy 'wid him ice-blue eyes' and the others like him; he recognises them and knowing them he knows how to play them.

The poem ends with a sardonic laugh. The persona 'confesses' 'if I get through I gone,/ gone from this bruk-spirit, kiss-me-arse place'. The poet summarises in these last two lines, the irony of the situation—the harsh realities for many in the Caribbean fuel the desire to leave home even if it is to the place where 'the Marine boy' lives.

Baugh uses Jamaican Creole, the 'heart language' of the people, to emphasise their plight, including an ambivalence to home. And the Creole nuanced as it is here not only evokes laughter (in the cathartic sense—see for example, the Jamaican saying, 'you tek serious tings mek joke') but also suggests the complexity of the situation.

'Home' is for the young man a 'bruk-spirit, kiss-me-arse place' and no doubt for many others like him the social and economic inequities force migration at any cost—even the disrespect and ostentatious power display in the visa section. Yet the visa section is a micro-cosm of the broader inequities that the migrant will face abroad. On the other hand, the young man's self-assurance, his obvious ability to 'read' the signs, to negotiate and to position himself away from the scrutiny of the ice-blue eyes reflects a certain possession of self. Such self-confidence must in some way be connected to his sense of home. And that is the point; home, despite its challenges, provides an identity and gives to the individual a spiritual connection to place. So the young man, despite his apparent dismissal of place, is taking with him knowledge of belonging somewhere, of possessing a language and in particular an ability to negotiate in other spaces. What the poem has helped us to understand is how one's place, notwithstanding its many limitations, is enabling.

These poems, by well-established Caribbean poets, have explored what constitutes the Caribbean homeland and how knowledge of this place provides an anchorage and power. Now we move on to the next generation of poets as they explore issues of violence, migration and the future of the region. Post-independent poets, they add new perspectives as they re-imagine and re-position the Caribbean region and its people in a wider world.

Kei Miller: 'How Quickly You Grow'

Kei Miller's poem, 'How Quickly You Grow', explores the extended Caribbean home, situated in the diaspora. It, in fact, addresses the other side to Baugh's poem; the visa is granted, the journey made and the migrant is settled in the new country. The voice of the persona differs from that of 'Nigger Sweat': Caribbean migrants are after all not a homogenous group, but their experiences would be similar in a number of ways. They would be engaged in creating home away from home.

The distinguished poet and scholar, Kwame Dawes, tells us that '[writers] must always be both at home and away from home. Exile is no longer the same . . . even when I was in Jamaica, I wrote of Jamaica as someone looking in' (Dawes 2007: 52). This question of exile is one that most Caribbean writers have had to confront and this has been discussed in Chapter 6. Migration is embedded in the Caribbean experience. The islander looks to the seas: 'The starved eye devours the seascape for the morsel/Of a sail' as Walcott wrote many years earlier (1969b: 9). Miller's poems provide this kind of insider/outsider perspective to which Dawes refers. The poem begins with a striking image of a meal:

> In this country, when you can't afford
> more than one tin of ackee
> you might use mushrooms to stretch the pot.
>   (Miller, 2007: 16)

It is an image that counters the popular migrant dream of abundance when journeys end in the industrialised North. The image also ironically points to what the migrant cannot really afford—a 'home'. However, the persona attempts to re-produce this as he transforms the Jamaican national dish of ackee and saltfish into tinned ackee and mushrooms. Desire for home is thus assuaged as the persona learns to adapt and to accommodate.

Accommodation and adaptation have been some of the strategies used by the colonised and the former colonised to survive the imperial presence/domination. Here in the imperial presence, in (t)his (new) country, the migrant is impelled to find creative ways to survive. Miller explores some of these in other poems as well. In the poem, 'You say bomboclawt softly', the persona recalls the 'forbidden' language of home—a kind of 'heart' language. Like spiritual tongues, the expletive, 'bomboclawt' is the sound created when no words can be found to express the deepest feelings. Or the migrant reaches for a form to connect with home, like the dance, even though at home that was not his art: 'In this country on a Saturday night/you are usually the best dancer/it was not so back home'.

But adaptation is often a yoking of disparate things as in 'ackee and mushroom'. The image jolts viscerally. The matter-of-fact tone further heightens the sense of dislocation of the migrant. The poet, however, offers the hybrid form as a way to locate self, to create one's place. Ackee and mushrooms when combined do not lose their distinct taste. The hybrid created does not mean a loss of identity. Yet there is distinction between creolisation and hybridity that provides another reading. (See earlier discussion on Scott's 'Guard-ring'.)

Tongue-in-cheek, the poet, moreover, suggests that hybridity is the 'new normal': 'Beware how quickly you grow/accustomed to this taste . . . ' Underlying the irony, however, is the poem's insistence on border expansions. The persona's island has not disappeared, home has not been abandoned. Home instead is positioned in the new country; the island borders have been expanded:

> I have not become British
> but my island has become wider.

There is a certain stillness, a hushed quality—produced by the use of the sibilants, as in: 'you might use mushrooms to stretch the pot'. It is almost as if the poet is whispering this new found knowledge to survive. What is suggested is an awareness of the danger of losing the self in the hybrid form and the possibility that the form once worn can never be shaken. 'How Quickly You Grow' not only alludes to the pace of adjustment in the new country but also to an accommodation that may lock one in a 'kumbla'[1] so that home and self are forever changed.

The title, 'How Quickly You Grow' repeated in the poem with its overtones of amazement and irony marks not only how easy it is to lose one's identity in the new country but also intimates that the new landscape provides other kinds of growth and development. In the new country after all you may, as the poet says, become a person who is likely to be interviewed.

In opposition to this, however, is the gentle insistence that accommodation in this way is not loss but a formless expansion of self and home. In the second stanza, framed by the interviewer's question, 'what is it like living here', the poet reinforces the image of 'the foreigner'. The question marks the persona as one who is from elsewhere. There is again the claim that the self is not lost; its distinctiveness still recognisable in the new place. Yet the last two lines, 'I have not become British/but my island has become wider', includes the thought, the fear perhaps, 'I have become British'.

Notwithstanding the meditative and self-reflective tone, the poem carries a warning—home even with its abundance, its ackee trees enough to feed a nation, could be seen as limiting from the migrant's new found perspective. What Miller has explored here is the migrant's recurring 'fear'—the loss of identity, a sea crossing that may make home unattainable. Yet there is no mistaking the insertion of home in the migrant's country. What Miller reveals is the complexity of representations of home. It is a complexity that Christian Campbell also addresses.

Christian Campbell: 'Iguana'

In an interview with Lisa Allen-Agostini about his first collection of poetry *Running the Dusk,* which won the best first collection prize at the Aldeburgh poetry festival, Christian Campbell makes the point that the 'Caribbean is shaped by error, rupture, violence' and that it is the 'poet's job, to figure and disfigure to stay in the break' (2013). In 'Iguana', Campbell does exactly that. He figures, disfigures and stays in the break as he plays with the idea of Guyana as Iguana—a stranger's error in referring to the country, a misnomer for Guyana. Campbell in addressing the outsider's perspective enlarges the representation of home in a distinct Caribbean space.

The poem opens on a comic note:

> My friend from Guyana
> was asked in Philadelphia
> if she was from 'Iguana'
>   (Campbell, 2010: 39)

Campbell in the same interview refers to 'Iguana' as 'a "found poem" in a sense'. At a conference in Philadelphia, a Guyanese friend (who lived in Toronto) confessed to him, 'I couldn't live here. Somebody asked me if I was from "Iguana"!' Campbell said he could not stop laughing, but then thought, 'This is ripe for the picking!'

Yet from that comic opening Campbell moves on to create a distinct sense of the region, reflecting as he does so his view of the Caribbean. The comic opening of course also recalls an earlier error, that of Columbus who thought that he had reached the East when he landed on Caribbean shores as well as the other errors and ruptures produced by that alleged 'discovery' of Columbus. The poem has a strong aural quality, which is very much responsible for the elegiac tone. Interestingly, Campbell sees 'Iguana' as a poem that 'embodies the way in which [his] work is as much elegy as it is etymology'. And 'Iguana' is an elegy; Campbell's exploration of 'Iguana', its meanings, its roots and its associations creates a poem that celebrates as well as 'grieves' for the Caribbean.

In opposition to the comic and even reductive scene of the stranger misnaming of Guyana, is the image of the iguana itself—an image of a powerful figure, at home in its place:

> Iguana, which crawls and then
> stills, which flicks its tongue at the sun.

And so begins the re-visioning and re-writing of Guyana and the rest of the Caribbean. The poem reads like a praise poem of the region as it displays the connectedness of these countries, their roots, their history, their vastness, the richness of their environment. The name 'Iguana' is revisioned as the poet plays with its different forms. It evokes Lucayans, recalling the original inhabitants of the Bahamas—and produces a sense of ancestry and of rootedness. And even as the poet sardonically recalls some of the misinformation of the history taught, such as that the Caribs ate Lucayans, he employs the myth to point to an elemental union of Caribbean peoples.

Interesting too is his use of the brackets. Information apparently unimportant is placed in brackets, almost as an afterthought to draw our attention to essential information about the Caribbean—its colonial history and its struggle for Independence, as imaged in the change of a name, in the movement from Guiana to Guyana. Guiana, the colony then, is Guyana—the independent country now. The geography of the islands is also mapped in these brackets:

> Guiana (the colonial way,
> with an i, southernmost
> of the Caribbean) is iguana; Inagua
> (southernmost of The Bahamas,
> Northernmost of the Caribbean)
> Is iguana—Inagua, crossroads with Haiti . . .

Thus the poet unveils the reach and diversity of the region. 'Iguana' is also treated as a symbol of the fertility of the islands: 'Heneagua/"water is to be found there," water, water everywhere'. The fruitfulness of the region, acknowledged by the first Spanish visitors, is emphasised as the poet recalls the even earlier Taino's appreciation of this fact:

> Guyana (in the language of Arawaks,
> Wai Ana, 'Land of Many Waters')
> is iguana, veins running through land,
> grooves between green scales.

But this praise poem of the Caribbean reads also like a 'remembrance'. Its elegiac quality grows even stronger as the poem ends in a refashioned couplet:

> And all the iguanas scurry away from me.
> And all the iguanas are dying.

The threatened Caribbean landscape is evoked. The image of the endangered iguana, with which the poem ends, suggests not only the present ecological losses but also a threatened Caribbean future. The poem ends on this note of certainty and pathos, so different from its opening comic and sardonic tone. Moreover, the poem's shifting mood from comic to celebratory and then to melancholy casts a shadow on the Caribbean future. Yet as Campbell writes in the poem titled, 'Robert Love Monument':

> Redemption coming, redemption coming,
> the half that has never been told.
> Lucaya arise and go to the harbour.
> Greet your ship, your ship
> of black and gold.

Redemption is possible; one is after all 'running the dusk'. In mapping Guyana this way Campbell illustrates the breadth of the region to suggest the complexity of what constitutes the Caribbean home.

Tanya Shirley: 'A West Indian Poem'

The poets discussed so far help us understand the shape of the Caribbean home. In addition to this, Tanya Shirley in 'A West Indian Poem' provides us with a vision of the arrival home, at Heartease. Her poem recalls Goodison's 'Heartease 1', which asks: 'How far is it to

Heartease?' and answers 'Just around the corner.' Shirley's poem represents this hope. To get there, however, the history of violence in the Caribbean has to be acknowledged and shown to be related to oppression, to an absence of justice and rights. Peter Tosh's insightful song, 'there can be no peace without justice' helps make transparent this connection.

> Perhaps tonight when the dream stealers
> are on the prowl,
>
> a dead bird's dried blood will remind them of God
> and we shall we passed over.
>
> (Shirley, 2009: 19)

But the poem is equally about the religious faith of a people that frees them from an oppressive system and helps them establish their own home. The parallel with the Israelites leaving Egypt to found their place in Canaan is clear. The poem in fact reads like a prayer but it is also very much a lament as Shirley both offers and questions the power of the religious faith of a people to create a home built on justice and equal rights.

The opening image of a bird smashing into a human construction is not unfamiliar. The poet's rendering of it as 'our house/has killed a bird' introduces the theme of injustice:

> It is not the first time our house
> has killed a bird

'Our house' may in effect be read as a metonym for all human constructs—material and mental—damaging human and non-human lives. The matter-of-fact tone belies and emphasises this. Yet there is no escaping too the personalised 'our house' or the title of the poem 'A West Indian poem', which particularises violence even as it universalises it. The use of the indefinite article in the poem's title flags this violence as embedded in the Caribbean landscape. 'It is not the first time . . . ' brings into focus the history of violence. And underneath the matter-of-fact tone of these opening lines is a tone too of regret and sadness.

The benign image of humans' violence as simply part of nature, is strikingly undercut with images of violence calculated and planned: 'the woman rising from her evening prayers/shot dead . . . '; 'the blood below the sea, the cotton, the sugar, the whip'. Thus the present violence is linked to a history of violence, of the Middle Passage, of slavery, of oppression. And in foregrounding the poem in that place, the poet alludes to persisting forms of economic, social and political oppression that have helped to produce this internal carnage—the latter so heart-rending that the matriarch is impelled to plead with 'the older spirits' for pardon for 'how we have wasted/the blood they fought to keep . . . ', for the blood they had spilled for freedom.

Ironically, the present blood-letting is as political as that of the colonial period. The freedom fought for and achieved is dismissed as the new 'massa', the new 'overseer', like the old, thinks nothing of 'the faces, each week more and more, in the Gleaner's obituary'. The contrasting images of violence point to the abuse and the reduction of a people by the 'dream stealers' who simply crave power. The latter image recalls Carter's poem 'This is the Dark Time My Love' in which the poet asks 'Who comes walking in the dark night time?' and answers, 'It is the man of death, my love, the stranger invader/watching you sleep and aiming at your dream' (Carter, 1989). The stranger invader then and now threatens any vision of freedom. What Shirley suggests is that the destruction of home is the work of outsiders or belongers who have become outsiders.

Juxtaposed against this violence is the religious faith of a people. Such faith is alluded to in the poet's use of the image of the bird-blood sacrifice, 'but that red smeared/like shield and omen'. The allusion is to that of the Jewish Passover narrative in which the blood of a sacrificed lamb was smeared on a doorpost as a sign to the avenging angel to pass over the oppressed Israelites. It is of course also an allusion to the essential tenet of Christianity—the sacrifice of the lamb, Christ, for one's salvation, for which the Jewish Passover tradition is seen as a signifier. The poet's re-visioning of the image of the blood of the lamb to the blood of a bird as a means to salvation challenges the idea of religious salvation. Moreover, 'that red smeared . . . ' is both shield and omen. The duality of violence—it protects but also destroys—makes even religious faith rooted in such violence troubling. The image 'shield and omen' aptly captures this duality. An omen is, after all, a prophetic sign with an ominous ring to it. Violence can destroy everything:

> but that red smeared
> like shield and omen
> sucked up all the sun, the breeze, the slopes,
> the trees, the colour.

In the next two stanzas the accumulation of select details reveals the intensity of the violence. The agents of these acts as well as their victims are nameless. Their namelessness suggests the extent of the violence but also an apparent insignificance connected to a sense of the absence of God. The half-rhyme linking prayers and obituary and the image of 'the woman rising from her evening prayers/shot dead . . . ' juxtaposed with 'a dead bird's dried blood will remind them of God', mark this apparent absence of God.

The poem ends seemingly on a note of hope but such hope appears foreclosed as the last image loops back to the 'woman rising from her evening prayers/shot dead in her house last night'. The quietly mocking tone of the poet as she equates 'a dead bird's dried blood' with that of the Lamb of God questions the meaning of religious beliefs. Furthermore, the phrase 'passed over' suggests not only the hope of the Passover but also the despair of being passed over/forgotten. Yet the bird image also recalls the passage from the gospel of St Matthew (10:29) 'are not two sparrows sold for a farthing? And not one of them shall fall on the ground without your Father caring.'

In contrast to this tentative hope is the certainty of the traditional authority figure of the grandmother, the matriarch, imaged (or imagined) as 'sitting with the older spirits'. The poet highlights this as she connects the slain woman (and by extension all the other deaths) with that of the matriarch, 'I thought of the woman . . . ', 'I thought of my grandmother . . . ' It is as if the poet is offering the folk tradition with the belief in 'The Mother' as the real hope. Or perhaps like Scott's poem, the poet is drawing on both the Christian as well as the folk tradition, even as she questions the basic tenet of Christianity, that of a caring God. A powerful poem, it reaches for a faith that will anchor the hope of salvation for the region, for arrival finally to 'Heartease'.

These representations of a Caribbean homeland show a distinctive culture despite the many incursions into that space. As a result of its specific traditions, languages and its creolised culture, which the poets in this chapter have all explored, this homeland has avoided being assimilated by western discourse, despite its dominance. The poets explore the major issues facing Caribbean society in the re-created space: violence, oppression, poverty, a threatened environment. Yet they also celebrate the beauty of the Caribbean landscape, the strength and courage of its people, their music and their faith. They signal a future filled with hope. Finely crafted poems, employing the language range of Caribbean Standard English and Creole, these poems so rooted in the Caribbean, speak to all peoples.

Note

1 Kumbla—this alludes to the Jamaican expression, 'go enna kumbla', which means to hide in a safe place. The kumbla however is a small space and even though it provides protection it can also seal one in. For a fuller exploration of the term see Brodber, Erna (1980) *Jane and Louisa Will Soon Come Home*. London: New Beacon Books.

Chapter 8

Teachers' voices

The responses of three groups of teachers, in three settings, to the teaching of Caribbean poetry

Beverley Bryan with Georgie Horrell
and Sandra Robinson

Introduction

The previous chapters have explored and expanded our understanding of Caribbean poetry, considering key themes, poets and issues. This was our first task; the second, the teaching task, we touched on in Chapter 5 as Pollard and Whitley explored their teaching of Walcott. We need to go further to examine the responses of the teachers we want to enrol on this project, to bring the wealth of Caribbean poetry to students. This chapter reports on some 'first takes', i.e. initial responses to this body of work as presented to teachers in different settings and our investigation to consider the attitudes of these groups of teachers towards poetry, its value to them, and their competence in teaching it.

Teachers' competence in teaching poetry

> Poetry matters because it is a central example of the use human beings make of the words to explore and understand.
>
> (Brindley, 1994: 211)

Benton (1999, 2000) reported on a country-wide survey of poetry teaching in the UK that considered how teachers viewed: (i) the reading and discussion of poetry; (ii) the writing of poetry; and (iii) the concerns they have about its delivery. He noted the evolution over a 16 year period in teachers' sense of competence in teaching poetry, from feelings of inadequacy to a growing competence and a more positive attitude towards the value of poetry. Benton reported on a change in the perception of poetry from being of:

> the highest value in encouraging students to think analytically, unravelling the complexities of this 'charged' language.
>
> (Benton, 1999: 525)

... to a broader concern with self-expression and diversity within the constraints of a National Curriculum. Nevertheless the teaching of non-British poetry presented some problems for a sizeable number of teachers stemming from:

> [a] lack of knowledge about the background and cultural assumptions behind the poems and, perhaps most strongly, from a lack of confidence when reading the poems, particularly those written in Caribbean Creole, aloud to classes.
>
> (Benton, 2000: 85)

More recently, Dymoke (2012) has noted an additional concern with the narrowing demands of the UK National Curriculum in English and the 'potential new tensions between assessment and creative opportunities' (p. 407). Nevertheless she invokes the power and value of poetry to widen students' experiences of the world outside the classroom and outside their own culture.

In the Caribbean, the case for the value of poetry can be strongly made, as demonstrated by the popularity of poetry festivals, the emphasis on lyrics in DJ sound clashes, the enduring support for calypso song competitions, the resurgence of Creole/Heritage day activities and the insertion of such as the recitation as performance, in routine school functions. As compelling is poetry's cultural and pedagogical value. In the Introduction to this book, we spoke of the varied language of Caribbean poetry as a defining characteristic but even as we explore the cultural benefits that we find in the poetry, we must also consider the pedagogical opportunities available to examine how 'charged language' works as patterning in texts. This is useful for Caribbean learners who are second language learners of English and in a bi/multilingual environment, the possibilities of meta-linguistic awareness offers the opportunity to pay conscious attention to language; to approach language as also meaning-charged; and to unpick language so that we can evaluate its effects. This has to be seen as one of the most significant aspects of the value of poetry in the Caribbean.

The state of poetry teaching throughout the Caribbean has come in for some attention through the Caribbean Examination Council (CXC), which is the regional body that is most preoccupied with the disciplinary expertise of Caribbean teachers. As with the situation in the UK, teachers are increasingly dependent on the examination board, drawing on it for advice and guidance on their teaching. The CXC has indicated some dissatisfaction with the delivery of poetry and the annual report on each year's examination offered a variety of comments as well as suggestions about how practice might be changed:

> Examiners noticed a widespread absence of any evidence that candidates were being taught to read poetry as a genre.
>
> (CXC, 2006: 6)

While in 2008:

> candidates responded with strong emotions to injustices presented in the poems. This enthusiasm is commendable, but it needs to be channelled into disciplined discussion of poetic devices that evoked such strong emotions.
>
> (CXC, 2008: 7)

Similarly, in 2010 there was an exhortation to move from a shallow engagement:

> they should be empowered to master the language to *describe, explain* and *analyse* with greater clarity those experiences shared and gained through listening and speaking.
>
> (CXC, 2010: 7)

The CXC reports suggest that there is engagement as the students 'responded with strong emotions', but the enrichment that needed to come from unpicking the language was missing. They are also looking at an interaction with poetry that will enhance the language of *description, explanation* and *analysis*. The focus on response was not as effective because students were not being guided to discover the depths of response possible. Similar critiques of poetry teaching have emerged from Her Majesty's Inspectorate (HMI) and Office for Standards in Education (Ofsted) Reports in UK in the last ten years, though they rarely acknowledge their own responsibility in the difficulties faced by teachers with numerous dictats coming their way on what should be taught and how it should be taught creatively.

Apart from the CXC reports, changing/emerging populations of Caribbean adolescents and the proliferation of new technologies are challenging teachers of English to greater accountability:

> their professional identities, their transparency of practice and how they represent their practice have consequences for what students are able to learn.
>
> (Hammerness et al., 2005: 358)

Thus collaboration has developed over the last two years to plan activities to enhance the knowledge and teaching of Caribbean poetry among secondary/high school students in the UK and West Indies through courses, workshops and research on teaching Caribbean poetry in the form of a Teaching Caribbean Poetry (TCP) course. What follows is one small part of the research aspect of the TCP project, which acknowledges the importance of poetry in language development, and in encouraging high order thinking and critical skills. It recognises the need for the continuing upgrading of our teachers of English in areas where there is insufficient support. It also recognises that improvements can be made as teachers examine their own experiences of poetry, analyse their responses to it and engage with new approaches and stances to poetry. The fact is that 'teachers attitudes to poetry are crucial in the importance they attach to it . . . and the way in which they demonstrate a concern and responsibility for it' (Brindley, 1994: 213).

The study and its methodology

This was the context of the research and the focus of the TCP project. It recognised that more could be done to enhance the teaching of poetry. Broadly, we wanted to promote achievement through learning and teaching of Caribbean poetry in schools in the Caribbean and UK. Specifically the course we designed supported teachers by expanding their knowledge base and developing their confidence with poetry as they inspire and educate their students. It thus sought to encourage and develop teachers' personal, analytical and pedagogical responses to Caribbean poetry. Such an evaluation of the teachers' response to the initiative can best be captured through joint research. Thus the aim of the investigation was to understand better the students' experiences with poetry, their attitude towards the subject generally as we introduced a unit of Caribbean poetry that would deepen enrichment and enhance engagement. The study covers three settings, namely Jamaica, the Eastern Caribbean and the UK. The course was offered in different ways while still covering the required content to varying degrees of detail. What follows are three accounts of the initial delivery and the teachers' responses. We will begin with Jamaica.

Jamaica

Forty (43) student teachers were involved in the study, coming from either the second year of a three year programme or the first year of a two year Bachelor of Education (B.Ed) programme. The three-year students had little or no experience of teaching, coming largely from high school. The two-year students came with some years of teaching and a teaching diploma gained at a teachers' college. We were concerned to gauge responses to the course and used a set of questions as a qualitative prompt, plus a quantitative Likert scale, as we knew that the nature of disposition and attitudes to poetry needed to be understood, measured and articulated in a quantitative as well as qualitative way.

Although we wanted to know how teachers responded to the course, we also wanted an assessment of their earliest experience with poetry. The majority of the responses from the qualitative prompts, some fifty-six per cent (56%), were largely positive, in terms of what the teachers said about their experiences of being taught poetry.[1] Most focused on school experiences that were personal and *emotional* with consistently recurring ideas of poetry needing to be always *relatable* and thus *allowed me to know my culture*. So context and content were seen to encourage *enthusiasm* and *motivation*. The *historical and sometimes post-colonial perspective* led to several references to *Colonial Girls School* by Olive Senior and other poets such as Derek Walcott, Lorna Goodison and Edward Baugh. Those students who were *mostly interested in the performance, the use of the vernacular* and *rhythm, enjoyed interesting and lively poems* that they read *lustfully* and which left them *smitten*.

The students who gave negative feedback of their experiences with poetry referred to it as being *quite dismal, hard to interpret* and *confusing* with *interpretation problems* leading to *monotony* that left them *fearful* of the whole experience. For one student, it was simply the case that Walcott *scares me*. The Nobel Laureate notwithstanding, usually the positive responses referred to the content, i.e. the poems and the poets. The negative responses on the other hand, highlighted problems that were firmly linked to bad classroom experiences, laid at the door of teachers who *do not dig deeper or challenge the students but expect them to write deeper*. The respondents took exception to the line by line analysis reminiscent of new criticism which increased the alienation from the genre: *a dull and boring teacher can knock excitement like a batsman hitting a 'six'*.

The course focused on two poets who are now on the Poetry Archive but who also functioned as teachers. Mervyn Morris, internationally acclaimed poet and Emeritus Professor of Creative Writing and West Indian Literature at UWI, Mona, was the first contributor. He taught the introductory unit under the title 'The Role and Scope of Caribbean Poetry'. The session covered issues/themes that included language (with 'A Tale of Two Tongues' by Earl McKenzie or 'How we became pirates' by Kei Miller); history and tourism with 'Residue' by Anthony McNeil; psychic integration with 'Broken Bowl' by Kendel Hippolyte; gender with 'Birdshooting Season' by Olive Senior; and Caribbean landscape and desire with 'Exile' by Geoffrey Philp. He also infused the exercise with his own personal involvement by offering alternative versions of one of his poems, *Eve (1)* and *Eve (2)*.

The other poet/teacher was Velma Pollard, also represented on the Poetry Archive, who is noted for her 1994 landmark publication *Dread Talk: The Language of Rastafari,* and several published collections of poetry, including *Crown Point and Other Poems* (1988), *Shame Trees Don't Grow Here* (1992) and *Leaving Traces* (2009). She had co-written the unit on Derek Walcott, and taught an introductory unit covering four of his poems, discussed in detail in Chapter 5.

Teachers' competence increased over the time of the intervention and this was noted by the course facilitator, Aisha Spencer, who helped to deliver the course:

> Students became more confident in speaking about the poems as the sessions went on, looking more closely at vocabulary, the 'manner of speaking' employed by the poet under consideration, the imagery in the poems, etc. It was clear that they had been opened up to a new way of seeing and indeed envisioning Caribbean poetry.

The quantitative data taken from the Likert questionnaires confirmed significant changes between the pre- and post-test. The improved results around the competence dimension were in areas of greater knowledge (*I do not know enough to teach Caribbean poetry*); leading to greater motivation (*I am stimulated when I think about teaching poetry*); increased confidence (*I feel competent when teaching poetry*); and less fear about the teaching of poetry (*Teaching poetry is one of the areas I fear most in the English curriculum*). The other dimension that was related to assessing the value of poetry showed little change. The positive attitudes remained high and constant for Jamaican teachers before and after the intervention. The table below illustrates:

Table 8.1 Table showing changes in Jamaican teachers' attitudes

Selected items from questionnaire	Level of agreement before intervention (%)	Response after intervention (%)
I do not know enough to teach Caribbean poetry	40	9
I am stimulated when I think about teaching poetry	51	69
I feel competent when teaching poetry	48	68
Teaching poetry is one of the areas I fear most in the English curriculum	48	35
Poetry teaching is worthwhile	98	100
Teaching poetry helps to develop students' thinking skills	100	100

Many teachers spoke of their increased confidence for a poetry *no longer viewed as boring and difficult.* Teachers who *never saw a difference between Caribbean poetry and the others* could now understand *the historical contexts, the literary devices and the biographical informa-tion . . . I feel much more enlightened and comfortable to approach the teaching of poetry . . .* There was firmer agreement that teaching poetry was a valuable teaching skill and one that helped to develop students' thinking skills, *able to facilitate students' concerns but also to foster great discussion and encourage individual critical thinking.* The course increased motivation as it provided the *techniques and strategies* so *I do not find the teaching of Caribbean poetry as tedious and mundane as I thought it was.*

The fear has gone: *I honestly had a phobia to poetry because I found it difficult to relate to some poems and thus gain a full understanding of them. And because of this, I really used to hate going to poetry class. However, now that I have gotten an insight into Caribbean poetry or poetry as a whole, I believe that my fears have gone somewhat . . .* For others the change was not so perceptible but worth recording: *My views have not necessarily changed. I would want to suggest that my views have been informed . . . there is no point living in the Caribbean and not learning how to teach our own Caribbean poems.*

The Eastern Caribbean[2]

In another part of the Caribbean, poetry teaching was also going on and in this section we explore the ways in which a selection of teachers from five territories in the Eastern Carib-bean articulated their attitudes towards the teaching of poetry and responded to the use of workshops in enabling professional development in the teaching of Caribbean Poetry. In total, approximately 190 participants from approximately 90 secondary schools and five Ministries of Education were registered, for these initial five workshops across the five territories. The participants' experiences varied considerably with regard to tenure, teacher training, and degree qualification and specialisation. Most were practising teachers who had experienced various approaches to poetry teaching as they progressed through their teacher training degree programmes and their Bachelor's degree programmes in English.

This time the TCP course was conducted in the form of workshops in St Vincent and the Grenadines, Barbados, Antigua and Barbuda, St Lucia and Grenada. The workshops were intended to offer a range of strategies and activities presented within the context of eight separate sessions, which were somewhat different from the scope of what was offered in Jamaica. The additional topics were the music of Caribbean poetry, the poem on the page (Walcott), the poem as performance (Braithwaite), women's voices (Goodison) and the CXC poetry syllabus, which is offered through the Council at the end of standard secondary education as the Caribbean Secondary Education Certificate (CSEC). Nevertheless, these workshops also included distinguished poets and teachers—Philip Nanton, Sam Soyer and Mark McWatt, Emeritus Professor of Literature at UWI, Cave Hill. In this way the consumers of the texts under discussion were sharing them with some of their producers and creators.

At the beginning and end of each workshop, participants were invited to complete the same Likert scale attitude survey that is mentioned above. Additionally, at the end of the workshop, participants were also invited and encouraged to respond to the evaluation instrument comprising nine open-ended questions, which invited their perceptions of the workshops as an approach towards the teaching of Caribbean poetry. The teachers' voices, emerging from this series of workshops, suggest that they require and desire ownership of classroom strategies and activities that can help them to effectively respond to the question: How best can my students engage with this poem? Their responses showed appreciation of contributions that were *interesting, inspirational and interactive,* providing assistance with teaching poetry at the lower levels as well as giving *a taste of how poetry should be read and taken more seriously.*

Offering practical experiences in workshops was another way of representing best practice: *the way in which we were given poetry in context encourages us to do the same in our classes.* It mirrored to teachers ways in which they could make transparent to their students how to value and engage with Caribbean poetry: *this course gave me a different insight to poetry. It changed my way of thinking, also my attitude towards the subject.* The teachers indicated that the workshop *boost[ed] my confidence in teaching poetry and the opportunity to embrace, admire and desire to emulate the facilitators of this workshop.* At the same time, as these models of practice were made explicit to the teachers, they learnt how to make their existing teaching routines in poetry more efficient and elaborated. *It was rewarding because I felt confident to explore my new found knowledge and apply it.* In fact, the ability to learn from others is central to teachers' adaptive expertise.

It is no secret that, in the Caribbean, most teachers of English at the secondary level use the CXC's CSEC syllabus for English as a curriculum guide and gravitate towards any experience that would enable their ability to negotiate this text for classroom practice: *reinforced some practice and shed some light on what CXC requires of students.* Still, as a whole most teachers spoke favourably about the TCP workshop as an overall good professional development experience. It was *fresh and informative and served as a refresher. Informative and it sparked my love for poetry . . . I realize that poetry is everywhere and can be expressed through music.*

At the end of the workshop teachers thought of poetry teaching as *stimulating, exciting* and *refreshing* and this is encouraging. Given the keenness of teachers' attitudes towards professional activities aimed at enabling their competence in the teaching of poetry, it can be concluded that any hesitation observed in teachers' move towards the teaching of poetry can be explained as an uncertainty not about the 'what' of teaching Caribbean poetry but rather about the 'how'. *I was able to put myself in the position of my students and experience their joys as they put pen to paper and compose their own poems.*

In spite of the overwhelmingly positive Eastern Caribbean response, there were some negative aspects that teachers commented on. Nearly all the participants agreed that the workshop needed to be extended over a longer period of time in order to facilitate a more intimate interaction with skills and knowledge. In fact, there were those who felt that the delivery, at times, was rushed and that too much material was being presented in too short a space of time. Teachers wanted the event *spaced over a longer period of time* with more time to reflect, internalise and participate in *activities in terms of writing poems*. A *follow-up* was required to allow for these review activities. The responses of the workshop teachers recognise that:

> Teaching requires that teachers come to think about (and understand) teaching in ways quite different from what they have learned from their own experiences as students.
>
> (Hammerness et al., 2005: 358)

The UK experience

The TCP course ran in 2011 as a CPD course at Cambridge Faculty of Education, taught by three contributors to this book with performances by John Agard and Dorothea Smartt. A number of teachers suggested on the initial Likert scale questionnaire that they did not feel confident about teaching Caribbean poetry—although they felt fairly positive and motivated about teaching poetry more generally. There was a general consensus that Caribbean poetry demanded a particular understanding of a range of Caribbean histories, geographies, environmental issues and uses of language. Most teachers who attended the course had been teaching for over five years and suggested that they believed that the poetry they taught was significant, even vital educational value to their pupils. The majority indicated that they believed strongly in the positive contribution to wider society that teaching poetry makes. Thus, although the course organisers may have anticipated applications from a cohort of teachers who were worried about teaching poetry in general, as Benton (1999) had indicated, it appeared that most who took the trouble to participate in this staff development initiative were already enthusiastic.

There were some similarities and some differences in the way the course was presented. Much of the content was the same as the other two settings, covering topics and themes mentioned earlier: the nature and scope of Caribbean poetry, music and language in Caribbean poetry; key poets such as Brathwaite, Walcott and Linton Kwesi Johnson. However, the course was delivered in a different way; there were two full days of lecture-seminars and as with other offerings there was exposure to poets. A 'twilight session' for discussion and consolidation was offered and attended by a number of the teachers. Further distance learning was also provided in the form of study material as well as supervisors allocated to each attendee to support self-study and enquiry. The course culminated in an assessed project written by attendees, which reflected their own response to the poetry encountered throughout the course, as well as the responses of their pupils to Caribbean poetry experienced in their classrooms. Again, there were some differences. The course provided some background knowledge of the Caribbean and Caribbean poetry, addressing particular details and empowering teachers to engage in meaningful ways with a range of poets from across the Caribbean.

The teachers' views and responses were captured in their journals and they appeared inspired, if a little daunted, by the perplexing use of language and the commensurate, thought-provoking ideas:

> In my previous experience of teaching Caribbean poetry, I would generally explain what dialect is and how this reflected the poet's identity, for example in John Agard's poem 'Half-Caste'. I did not consider that Nation Language existed or that it was linked to the African heritage of the Caribbean people and therefore deserving of mention.

Although post-colonial theory and its challenges were addressed only through the poetry itself, this field of provocative views somewhat divided the course participants into those for whom this was extraneous and irrelevant and those for whom this was indeed the heart of the matter when reading and teaching Caribbean poetry. Similarly, the problematised consideration of the reader as 'cultural tourist' was seen both as a stimulating and a deeply challenging notion. However, as one teacher noted, consideration of Caribbean history proved to be a crucial intervention:

> One of the key ideas that I gathered from the course on teaching Caribbean poetry was the historical context of the Caribbean people and how this influenced the writing . . . the poetry seems to encapsulate the absolute beauty of the islands and the violent history that has given birth to a vibrant, unique culture.

The influence of music on Caribbean poetry (and indeed of poetry in Caribbean music) allowed a productive discussion of both rhythm and history, and linked the poetry carefully to social responses to art. Understanding this link is explicated by this teacher's response (as described in her teaching journal):

> Being a fan of Kamau Brathwaite, I was very excited when I found the poem 'Calypso' which captures the quintessential spirit of the Caribbean as well as the rhythm. As a backdrop to teaching the beat of the poem, I considered that it would be important to focus on the musical instruments that go into Calypso music. The lesson was created to bring to life the passion and the intrinsic sensuality and vibrancy of the skin drums, bamboo sticks and rattles that match the sound of the lines of the poem and highlight its meaning. Brathwaite is a master of his art as he disparagingly ignores the common use of the iambic pentameter in English literature (which he equates to colonial oppression) and instead uses dactyls.

Environmental issues were considered throughout, particularly in relation to the landscape of the islands described in poems by Edward Baugh and Derek Walcott. Attendees responded with interest to ideas that are clearly crucial—and global—with a heightened sense of the issues at stake in Caribbean poetry and its potential in the British classroom. One teacher asserted,

> Caribbean poetry has been at once an evocative and a provocative journey for me both as a student and as a teacher. Despite having taught Caribbean poetry before, this course

gave me a deeper understanding into what makes Caribbean poets tick; it felt like I had begun reading a book from the third chapter and now I have had the opportunity to start from the beginning.

Like the teachers in the Eastern Caribbean, UK teachers did find aspects of the course challenging, perhaps most particularly the concept of 'nation language' and the employment of Jamaican Creole by such poets as Linton Kwesi Johnson. Responses to this session in particular suggested that a small number of the teachers would have preferred the provision of lesson plans and of resources for direct use in the classroom, rather than what was perhaps a difficult consideration of how a British teacher might engage with the vernacular offered in the poetry. Such discussions initiated the particularly thoughtful consideration of cultural tourism referred to earlier.

Evaluating responses

What has been described above are three initial responses to three different instances of our Caribbean poetry course delivered in three different settings. What can we say that they have in common? First, before we look for commonalities we must acknowledge and celebrate difference. It is inevitable that these teachers come to these events with a range of individual and collective experiences. Teachers in Jamaica responded quite differently to the issues of history and language. They embraced the opportunity to engage with issues from their own cultural context. The Eastern Caribbean teachers also appreciated the cultural content but seemed pre-occupied with the pressures of the examination system. The UK teachers were excited yet challenged by contradictions of history and language they encountered through the course. It reminds us again of the importance of context and the deeply situated nature of engagement—contingent and mediated by our own histories and culture.

In spite of the differences, the teachers demonstrated great interest in the political, historical and cultural content. In Jamaica, this was noted as a critical factor in securing Caribbean students' responses by poets who made full use of distinct Caribbean realities, portraying particular images, characters, situations or ideas about Caribbean forms. Familiar scenes and landscapes, the historical and cultural memory, were vital to developing a meaningful understanding of Caribbean poetry, as one facilitator noted. At the same time, she cautioned that teachers should be careful not to 'over-romanticise' Caribbean poetry, particularly because this would tend to isolate students even further from the desire to read and respond openly, without pre-conceived notions. One UK teacher noted:

> The first thing that strikes me is the power of the personal. If Linton Kwesi Johnson managed to speak directly to me as a 13 yr old then he is more than capable of making connections with the 13 year olds in my school. The Caribbean poets are exploring one of the world's most powerful narratives.

Another important aspect was the involvement of the poets in all three settings and the possibilities presented for making poetry more accessible and, in some sense, more democratic. This initiative increases the important performance element and focuses on the sound features that help students to visualise the content of the poem. If the poets are not available, other modalities can be substituted: the use of the Poetry Archive, which includes information about the poets as well as orally performed poems and ideas for classroom use;

YouTube; multimedia including DVD, cassette or CD players, where students listen to and watch interviews with poets. A click on Google can open up a world of information in video and sound. These are ways to assist in creating the textured world of the poem.

The third point noted was the teachers' interest and enjoyment in the exploration of the language. Specific uses of language familiar to the Caribbean students and the distinct Caribbean voice heard through insertions of Creole or of 'a way of speaking' that was unique to a particular Caribbean territory helped in understanding. They gave the attention required for understanding the deployment of sound, rhythm and intonation in the readings of Caribbean poetry; discussing it in phonological terms helped to enhance meaning and offered an appreciation of a distinctive form. In the UK setting, the poets' use of language was found more challenging but was eventually accepted as critical to understanding many poems.

Finally, all teachers saw the possibilities available for engaging students with Caribbean poetry, and thus exhibited a very positive self-efficacy, i.e. a high level of optimism about the possibility of using poetry to achieve significant results. The strategies and issues involved in realising those expectations will be the subject of our final chapter.

Notes

1 Teachers' and student teachers' quotes in response to questionnaires are in italics.
2 The poetry workshops in the Eastern Caribbean were magnificently organised by Sandra Robinson and Karen Thomas. In 2013, further workshops were conducted in Dominica, St Kitts and Nevis (including Anguilla and Montserrat) and Guyana. Sharon Phillip organized additional workshops in Trinidad and Tobago. In total, 370 teachers from ten ministries of education in the Caribbean benefitted from the initiative.

Chapter 9

Conclusion

Teaching Caribbean poetry

Beverley Bryan with Lorna Down, Roz Hudson and Aisha Spencer

There can be no question that Caribbean poetry is a dynamic, substantial and vital body of literature that can and does inspire teachers and pupils. In this final chapter we focus on our main objective: secondary school children's engagement with Caribbean poetry and how best to promote this.

Contemporary experiences of teaching Caribbean poetry

Little empirical work has been done on the teaching of Caribbean poetry—or, indeed, poetry in general. Our aims always included supporting teachers to feel more confident about tackling *any* poetry in the classroom. Scafe (1989) drew attention to a level of apprehension noted by teachers approaching Caribbean poetry twenty years ago, which we are pleased to report appears very different today. As noted in Chapter 8, Benton (1999) also reported on the evolution of more positive attitudes towards the teaching of poetry generally; although Caribbean poetry continues to create specific anxieties among teachers because of nation language, pronunciation and the importance of voice. We believe that the Caribbean Poetry Project in general, and the Teaching Caribbean Poetry (TCP) course in particular, has helped to move forward on these, and other, issues, inspired partly by the shared vision we have been able to develop, working in tandem from both Caribbean and UK perspectives.

Tessa Ware, senior teacher and Head of English at Alexandra Park School, Haringey, London at the time of writing, was both a member of the Advisory Panel and a participant in the first UK course run by the TCP project. She offers a very positive model of what can be achieved in this area. Her careful evaluation of her own initiative, contextualised through observations as to how Caribbean poetry is now viewed and used by teachers in her school setting, provides an invaluable insight into the challenges faced, but also what can be achieved. She identified some of the key issues that teachers grapple with, in terms of the different experiences and forms of English that might be encountered in the UK English classroom. The English classroom, as has been noted before, is a site of primary significance for 'accommodating difference, for contemplating and creating complex readings of self in relation to others in society . . .' (Bryan, 1995: 42), even though in terms of poetry teaching, this potential is currently being squeezed through a focus on a narrow content and mechanistic assessment targets (Dymoke, 2012). Ware bravely takes on the broader original humanistic task, exploring the English person's dilemma teaching Caribbean poetry in her 2012 classroom, where she was keenly:

> aware of my position in relation to these texts as a cultural 'tourist', exploring the poetry of a region I had no direct experience of.

She echoes the words of Stewart Brown (2007), who confesses his initial concerns with being caught up in this 'tourist/intruder gaze', but who eventually resolves that contradiction through personal engagement and considered self-criticism. Morag Styles also writes:

> Every so often, I get a sense of discomfort being a non-Caribbean person running a Caribbean poetry project. Although I've loved and promoted this poetry for many years, I recognize my limitations as a cultural 'tourist', exploring the poetry of a region of which I am an outsider, despite having many Caribbean friends and colleagues. This is probably no bad thing, as it helps me understand the position of many Caribbean poets living overseas, who also have feelings of not quite belonging.

Ware, too, sees this outsider gaze reflected in some poems of Walcott (for example 'The Light of the World') and Johnson (for example 'Reggae fi Dada'), picking up on the diaspora condition of alienation as both insider and outsider. She notes the attention to a range of voices in Caribbean poetry, and the complexity of response this necessarily engenders. This honest and open discussion allowed us to appreciate the kinds of understanding she had to develop in herself, before she could successfully lead her students to engagement with Caribbean poetry. Working with her colleague Crispin Bonham-Carter, who had developed a scheme of work on Caribbean poetry delivered to Year 8 students (aged 12–13), she was initially surprised to see that he had included some quite challenging poems in the scheme. Even participants on the TCP course had initially found it difficult to understand some of the poems selected, notably Linton Kwesi Johnson's 'If I Woz a Tap-Natch Poet', Michael Smith's 'Mi Cyaan Believe It' and Velma Pollard's 'Beware the Naked Man Who Offers You a Shirt'. Earlier critics often complained that teachers' choice of Caribbean poems could be largely expedient, as an instrument of classroom control rather than for their inherent quality, especially where black students predominated (Stone, 1981). It is interesting, therefore, to see how a representative group of north London students, attending a multi-ethnic comprehensive school in 2012, responded to this small-scale piece of action research. Ware and Bonham-Carter's findings will be referred to from time to time in this chapter.

A caveat

In moving towards our suggestions for teaching, one caveat is offered repeatedly by poets who themselves teach poetry. Cooke and Thompson (1980) interviewed a number of well-known poets for their alternative perspectives. It was notable that these poets privileged certain core values when teaching students: 'Getting them to enjoy the voice and the word . . . the whole bodily experience of the poem taking over' (134–5); liberating the 'intuitive magician-mind' (135); listening to poetry; students writing poetry; exposing them to the human being, the poet; exploring the physicality of poems. 'The emphasis on language as sound is the only way for students to fix the poem in their bodies, as well as organise its meaning in their minds' (140). The idea is to treat analysis with some circumspection, because sometimes a poem can work without a search for a symbolic meaning; sometimes the meaning is just there in what the poem does—in the creation of an experience and an evocation of feelings. Experience is all: distilled and patterned in language.

Cross-cultural approaches to teaching Caribbean poetry

With that pre-emptive warning in mind, we can now offer some of the ideas garnered before and during this project. First, and especially as a cross-cultural enterprise, we have to state that, when introducing students to Caribbean poetry, the construction of a multi-faceted context is critical. Aisha Spencer who taught the first Caribbean group in Jamaica adds: 'Students might be introduced to aspects of the Caribbean through documentaries; by visiting cultural heritage websites of the particular islands via the internet; by engaging with historical literature, newspaper clippings, certain radio and/or television programmes focused on the landscape and reality of the Caribbean.' It is the kind of painstaking exploratory work that English teachers carry out as they teach Shakespeare or the War Poets or Irish poetry. One part is the physical environment that the teacher invokes as a context for exploration—the experience and understanding of the Caribbean landscape that infuses the poetry. This is not an invitation to 'voyeurism' as a tourist but it is a first step in connecting to the 'muse' that drives the poetry. It is now possible using internet sources to find the geographical and background information that locates the poems as David Whitley showed in Chapter 1 and Crispin Bonham-Carter outlines in his approach to the scheme of work for 12–13 year olds:

> I start by asking the students to pinpoint the Caribbean on a world map . . . very few successfully identify individual islands . . . almost all the class tell me that the Caribbean is a hot and desirable holiday location . . . more detailed background knowledge is emerging and I hear students discussing hurricanes, floods and isolation alongside the previous idealised image of beach life.
>
> I give them a cloze activity based on Walcott's 'Midsummer Tobago'. Students have to locate Walcott's adjectives by the nouns they think they are most likely to be describing . . . Next I ask them to rewrite the poem using Walcott's structure, but considering their own environment in London in January.

Images of Tobago, with its beautiful landscape, are available for a discussion of Walcott's 'Midsummer Tobago' or Roach's 'Love Overgrows a Rock'. Similarly, the historical backdrop to limbo dancing, beyond the tourist attraction, is available on YouTube to support an exploration of Brathwaite's 'Limbo'. In fact, one teacher from the first UK course shared how she mirrored and adjusted a course session on the environment to include internet sources, although she ignored Roach's evocation of the island as also an emotional prison:

> it was imperative that I began with a lesson that showed them the geographical location of the Caribbean islands to begin with. The lesson offered facts, historical information and a YouTube video of someone sailing around the Caribbean Islands. This offered students an opportunity to actually see the places that the poets were talking about and to appreciate the immense sacrifice a lot of the Caribbean people made when they gave up their homeland to live overseas. There was definitely an avid appreciation of the lush verdant landscape as indicated by the emotional interjections of praise offered by the students. This prepared them for Eric Roach's poem 'Love Overgrows a Rock' where he refers to the island he lives on as a 'rock' and effectively describes it as 'foreground green; Waves break the middle distance'. Students were able to easily visualise the environment Roach is describing as they had already seen the amazing Caribbean beaches and could feel the powerful draw of the island.

Technology does offer assistance, and again teachers contribute by bringing their own experiences; choosing the poems that genuinely appeal to them; and opening up in an honest way to the responses activated by the readings. However, when all of the background work is done, it is the individualised identities and ideologies that the students bring to the texts that lies at the heart of a genuine response. What we would hope to achieve is for students to see the poems as problematising the often rather stereotypical images to be found through internet resources which are only valuable if used in the right way.

Reader response approaches to teaching poetry

In turning to the second part of the context however we are, of course, moving into the major area of response, a powerful and enriching approach. Louise Rosenblatt was one theorist who brought reception theory into the literature classroom.

> Each reader draws on a reservoir of linguistic and life experiences. The new meaning, the literary work, whether poetic or non-poetic is constituted during the transaction between reader and text.
>
> (Rosenblatt, 1991: 60)

Response depends on individuals, comprised of attitudes and ideologies, based on their own experiences, and mediated by the wider context of society. The meaning (and response) is constructed in the interaction between the reader and the text. This is critical in Caribbean poetry where the possibility exists for visceral and harrowing responses to experiences far outside the normal range offered in classrooms. In an article in *English in Education*, Bryan (1995) described such encounters and some of the results, showing how teachers have to find practical ways of guiding responses at different levels and in different ways.

Activating levels of response

The aim here is to differentiate response (Pappas, 1990) and to find pedagogical ways of structuring the engagement with activities that trigger different levels of response to classroom activities over a period of time. All levels do not have to be included but are dependent on how the poem fits within a unit of work. An *experiential* trigger would allow students to consider the first immediate response, sharing what is distinctive in the poem. The *connective* response tries to link what is created in the poem with the experiences of the reader. Tess Gallagher, an American poet, says in Cooke and Thompson (1980) that 'you have to stop referring everything immediately to the poet's life. Instead you bring it to your own life, and you're less frightened or mystified by it . . . ' (134). At the *analytic* level the kind of direction required is to look at how the poem works. This is related to the linguistic clues in the poem but as we are paying attention to poets, we note their wariness of critics (Showalter, 2003) and their focus on the word and the sound of the poem. They speak of enjoying the voice with the emphasis on language as sound and the physicality of poems. At an *interpretive level* the reader seeks meaning in the text. If there has been an earlier connection, then some kind of understanding becomes possible: 'people need to supply their own "*you's*", so when the poet says "you" they won't be so worried about the poet's *you* that they won't add their own' (137). A further development is *evaluative*, as the reader assesses the value of the effort extended. Throughout the reader's engagement, there should be *self-reflective* questions as students monitor their own responses and the quality of the interrogation.

Lorna Down recommends the use of Dennis Sumara's theory and practice of literary engagements (2002), which is another set of tools for 'digging deeper'. This approach to reading and responding to a poem is also activated over a period in which students have time to relate other materials and experiences to the poem. Recording their feelings in a journal, perhaps, and noting differences in their responses will allow for deeper reflection on the poem. This approach involves a number of steps:

1   *Read,* reflect and respond to the poem by making annotations. These annotations may take the form of underlining, circling words, writing comments on the poems as students respond to ideas that surprise, disturb, challenge and resonate with them.
2   *Share* these annotations with others.
3   *Listen* to the poet; read the poem if possible (the Poetry Archive is a valuable resource). Then return to the poem and in a different coloured ink record responses.
4   *Reread* the poem after a period of time has passed, a few days or a more extended period. Continue to make annotations. See if there are changes you wish to make. Refer to your life experiences, events in your society that relate to the poem. Now write these new comments in a different colour ink.
5   *Examine* other extra-textual material in class. This could include a pictorial representation of some aspect of the poem; a recording of a poem with a similar title or subject being said aloud or read, for example, on YouTube; a poem with a similar theme, a prose extract related in theme to the poem, headlines from a newspaper among other things. View/listen to/read these. After doing so return to the poem and again make annotations using a different colour ink.
6   *Share* your annotations with the class. The class begins also to construct its own 'personal' meanings.
7   *Reflect* on the changes in the comments that have been made throughout. Note the insights that emerge.

All of the above sets of responses can be achieved through discussion and deep reflection, but the most creative parts will be where students generate and present their own meanings. The concept of multiple intelligences can help direct the teacher to provide a range of activities in mixed media that take account of the different orientations of the students. Activities can be oral with a performance continuum that begins with simple recitations at one end, moving to sound, movement and drums and then to choral group drama at the other end. Often the very physicality of the poem will assist in understanding. Throughout this book, the oral and the performative have been highlighted by poets, teachers and students. This is because the poetry is embedded in the oral tradition through popular communication with, and the investment of, the audience (Breiner, 1998). All the poets work through a polyphony of voices from which they choose, whether it is Mikey Smith emphasising the importance of the sound of poetry and the rhythms of speech in an interview with Mervyn Morris or Eddie Baugh reminding us that all poems exist as performances of sound, manifested in voice. Kei Miller confirms these views in a Facebook entry: 'poetry is a kind of music . . . words are sounds . . . and a poem that doesn't rise off the page is in fact a dead poem' (2012).

Teachers in the UK who are working on Caribbean poetry for the first time, would be advised to access readings by Caribbean poets through the online Poetry Archive or listen to CDs of their work. Pupils of Caribbean heritage may be willing to read poems aloud and Caribbean poets can be invited to schools with many schemes available to help with costs. However, teachers should practice reading the poetry aloud themselves as difficulties with the printed version are often cleared up and because most Caribbean poetry comes to life with performance as demonstrated in Bonham-Carter's closing parargraph of his assignment:

> I want to end the course with a sense of celebration and participation. We watch John Agard performing 'Mr Oxford Don'. They love it and identify in Agard's performance all the performance ideals (enthusiasm, volume, rhythm, gesture) . . . I divide up Michael Smith's 'Mi Cyaan believe it' . . . the room is filled with energy, students standing on chairs, waving their arms, drumming rhthyms and celebrating the sounds of the poem.

A teacher of Jamaican heritage from the UK group related her experience of teaching Linton Kwesi Johnson's 'Inglan' Is a Bitch' and described using a YouTube reading by Johnson to enhance her lesson with a group of mixed ability, mixed heritage fourteen year olds:

> Pupils could pick up on the rhyme and rhythm and suddenly the fact that he was swearing was no longer important; it was what he was saying and how he was saying it that mattered. I could see on their faces that they liked the poem and the poet because he was fiery. In addition, they seemed to admire the fact that he was standing up in defiance against England and all of her injustices.

In pursuing the performance elements teachers might consider basing dance and drama around Lorna Goodison's 'Mother the Great Stones Got to Move' where some background material on revivalism in Jamaica would help in understanding, or Mikey Smith's 'Mi Cyaan Believe it', which is available on YouTube. Tessa Ware also discusses the usefulness of students' own performance in poetry and gives a number of reasons why they found it so animating:

- They enjoyed it—both performance in general and 'speak[ing] like a Caribbean person'.
- It helped them to understand the 'emotions' in the poem by considering how to read certain lines—this enabled them to get at the 'meaning' of the poem.
- It helped them consider how to engage with an audience and which features of performance would help them to do this. As a result, they could 'bring the poem to life' and 'feel the proper sense and rhythm of that poem'.

Ware quotes John Gordon (2004: 98) who has written of the way in which poetry is often studied in school as a purely written medium, blaming 'assessment arrangements that present poetry encounters as silent, individual acts in realms of print' and noting that, as a result, 'the orality of poetry is sometimes overlooked at the point of first encounter with any given text'. Gordon adds that, 'Dealing with the sound element of poetry means making utterance public, rendering poetry social, a collective act'. It is fitting that students most enjoyed the activity that brought them closest to the oral, performative elements of Caribbean poetry.

In spite of what has been said about oracy, writing can be another creative avenue for response, liberating what in Cooke and Thompson is the 'dreaming-mind, your intuitive magician-mind' from 'the organizer-mind' (1980: 135). There is an echo here of Britton's participant/spectator dichotomy employing language for different purposes (Britton 1984) or Rosenblatt's (1991) aesthetic/efferent distinction in literature; separating the transactional function of involvement with the world from the poetic stance where words are employed for their own sake. The production of text is what is being encouraged—where students become poets themselves, using some of the easier forms they are introduced to, to create their own texts. We can take as one example Whitley and Bonham-Carter's suggestion from 'Midsummer Tobago' to use Walcott's own lines:

> Broad sun-stoned beaches.
> White heat.
> A green river . . .

and then ask students to write their own parallel sequence of images of heat (or cold!) centred on their own experiences and sense of place. Another example might be the use of Fred D'Aguiar's 'Mama Dot' title poem:

> Born on a Sunday
> in the kingdom of Ashante
> . . .
> Freed on Saturday
> in a new century

Pupils may be familiar with the traditional Solomon Grundy rhyme and use it as a template to come up with their own lines for each day of the week. The original introduces the painful issue of slavery which is in the background of most Caribbean poetry, but in an accessible way, rooting the poem back to Africa in the first line yet ending with a note of hope.

Communicative strategies for teaching poetry

The suggestions for creative writing above do not mean that the transactional cannot be used in some units. Communicative activities would allow students who have been fully immersed in the experience of the poem to demonstrate that understanding in another mode or genre. We can take as example one piece of homework given by Ware and Bonham-Carter, after the study of their unit:

> *Imagine a newspaper has criticised modern schools for teaching Linton Kwesi Johnson's poetry. Write a letter to the editor of the newspaper explaining why you think it is important to study poetry in different dialects.*

Only if the students have responded and engaged in some of the ways detailed above could they deliver this piece of writing with success, as indeed they did. If students organised a bigger speech event such as a themed assembly based on Caribbean poetry, or their own poetry 'conference', a range of genres of texts and speech events would be employed. Responses to poetry can be presented through journals, posters, logs, prayers, memos, speeches, dictionaries, glossaries, class wikis etc.

Lorna Down suggests some communicative activities that could follow a study of certain poems. She suggests that students select images of the landscape that are presented in Olive Senior's 'Meditation in Yellow' (2005) and have them match these with actual photos/images of the Caribbean landscape. A powerpoint presentation with the lines of the poem accompanying the selected photos/images produced by the students can be an engaging activity. This kind of activity could be extended using music and drama developed around a poem or series of poems. The environment is one theme that fits well within Caribbean preoccupations and is a rich and constant source of imagery in the poetry.

A communicative focus will also encourage oral work as noted above. The content of Caribbean poetry lends itself to discussion of topics such as gender or identity, and others such as tourism, climate change, migration, community rights etc. These can be presented through a variety of media and usefully linked with other types of texts—both fiction and non-fiction. The students can be given opportunities to compile their own anthologies for occasional readings; or discuss the merits of well-chosen poems through paired work, whole class discussions or debates. Again the oral output could involve responding to a range of oral forms or speech events that shape Caribbean poetry—such as an interview, speeches, sermons, soliloquy etc.

Language awareness strategies for teaching poetry

Another rich and productive seam to be mined for teaching Caribbean poetry is that of linguistics. It is the case that linguistic analysis can sometimes come too soon (see Whitley on Walcott) if we analyse before we are moved or engaged. What we want to introduce in this discussion of language in Caribbean poetry would not be the dry attention to linguistic items such as syntax—rather we would be concerned, first, with semantics in that moving/inspirational sense as we try and understand the driven pursuit of poets such as Kei Milller (2010) in the search for the perfect word:

> and the poem will not care that some walk past
> afraid of the words we try out on our tongues
> hoping this finally is the language of God
> that he might hear it and respond

This type of semantic activity can be undertaken with a wide range of poetry. What is unique to Caribbean poetry are the cadences of the oral tradition and culture, offering styles and forms that students could imitate. Dub poetry is one form that might be popular with secondary students, because of its rhythm, its topical content and interesting use of nation language. Use can also be made of reggae songs for analysis and comparison—to see how language works in presenting Dawes' argument about a distinctive aesthetic from established poets such as Marley or Tosh to insurgents such as Bounty Killa ('Experience') or Babycham ('Ghetto Story'). If we were to go further into the music, the rhymes and puns of the good DJ demand a reservoir of skill and metalinguistic awareness not often acknowledged. Additionally, the alternative African voice found in kaiso (or calypso) provides another avenue for exploration of the wordsmith and the purveyor of puns, both lewd and political. We have already linked the Mighty Spoiler with Derek Walcott but the rich emphasis of calypsos on narrative form and language play provide a good resource for not only teaching poetry but also for analysing narrative structure and creolised forms. Some calypso content is highly sexualised but suitable topics can be found for relevant age groups that would allow history, politics and culture to become rhythmically available. In so doing, a link can be made to comparable English and American ballads, and to extension work using story boards, drama and film production.

Language play can also be serious language study. Bryan (2010) suggests the use of 'Reggae fi Dada' by Linton Kwesi Johnson, 'Uncle Time' by Dennis Scott, 'Albert' by A.L. Hendriks and 'Speechify' by Louise Bennett, as a group of poems for language study. After time for discussion and in-depth responses to the poems, a group of teachers were asked to arrange them on a continuum from the most Jamaican to the least, with linguistic justification for the choices made.

> At one level, we would have looked at these texts as literature but as these are all poems that draw on the Jamaican language, the vernacular is seen as being given serious consideration. The students will also need to know some of the rules of Jamaican, to see which poem makes most use of them.
>
> (Bryan, 2010: 100)

Bryan describes poetry as 'the best home for language study' and went on to discuss using the poems to privilege nation language; to discuss language change through history and migration; and to acknowledge the acquisition process made possible by language contact. She also suggests comparing vernaculars in different territories, so comparisons can be made: for example, Kwéyòl in such as Walcott; Guyanese Creole continuities in John Agard; Barbadian Creole in Brathwaite and in a British-born Barbadian such as Dorothea Smartt; leading to new 'crossings' (Rampton, 1995) in the diaspora.

Final words on teaching Caribbean poetry

The work of Tessa Ware, Crispin Bonham-Carter and other teachers suggest that our enterprise to encourage the teaching of Caribbean poetry across these different settings has been entirely worthwhile. Tessa Ware's students also showed an interest in the language. She questions whether dialect is seen so pejoratively now, when speakers with a range of English regional dialects feature regularly on the BBC with global exposure. She found that a real depth of understanding, interest and engagement in language could result from looking at Caribbean varieties, as her students revealed. These were some of their responses to the communicative exercise in defence of Creole poetry:

> If we no longer teach Caribbean poetry in our school then pupils will not understand the different ways of Caribbean culture and Caribbean pupils will find it an offense that there poems are not good enough to read when they are.
>
> So what's a little difference in language, in the end we will understand the message of the poem.
>
> the informal writing that is used can have a more interesting effect on the reader. For instance, the reader could try to independently work out what Linton Kwesi Johnson is saying in the poem, and as a result the person is thinking carefully about his poetry.
>
> the effect it gives [of] the poet him/herself. What I mean by this is the way the words would be spelt and pronounced when reading it really builds up the poet's identity.

There was something about Johnson's assertion of his own alternative Creole voice that persuaded the whole class that this was an important aspect of poetry. They showed a fundamental understanding that the language used 'encodes' culture in some way and were critical of implied value judgements. Students were very much aware of the 'code-switching' involved in the poets' deliberate appropriation of Creole, and the reasons for it. The insights yielded by these students represent a trenchant argument for Caribbean poetry as a way of encouraging tolerance of difference, enhancing language awareness and developing high-level thinking skills.

But beyond this, as we have argued throughout this book, Caribbean poetry embodies qualities that make it potentially a uniquely valuable experience for young readers. Caribbean poetry's strong connection to oral and performative traditions give it vital energy and accessibility; its organic links with the region's popular musical culture make it alive to the rhythms of ordinary life; its historical role as an expressive medium resisting oppression imbue it with an inner strength and power. Caribbean poetry is celebratory, as well as an agent for critical social consciousness; its home ground is one of the most beautiful places on earth, rendered vulnerable by environmental change, entrenched in poverty, and witness to some of the darkest episodes in modern world history. These paradoxes give Caribbean poetry its distinctive charge, making it an especially potent manifestation of the key qualities that run through all poetry, which it is vital young learners have an opportunity to experience in depth. This is a body of poetry that has the capacity to be, in Walcott's compelling phrase, the 'light of the world'. Our book makes a small, but we hope significant, contribution to widening awareness of the importance of Caribbean poetry and to ensuring that teachers are well equipped to make children's engagement with it as rich as possible.

> And may your portion be song
>   Whose notes never die
> And may the music be sweet,
>   Goodbye.
>   Kei Miller

Bibliography

Adisa, O.P. (1992) *Tamarind and Mango Woman*. Toronto: Sister Vision Press.

African Caribbean Institute of Jamaica (2013) 'Revivalism in Jamaica': www.anngel.com/ACI history-revivalism.htm (accessed 15 February 2013).

Agard, J. (1984) *I Din Do Nuttin*. London: Bodley Head Children's Books.

——— (1985) *Mangoes and Bullets: Selected and New Poems, 1972–1984*. London: Pluto Press.

——— (1996) *Get Back, Pimple!* London: Viking.

——— (2007) 'Checking Out Me History': http://www.poetryarchive.org/poetryarchive/singlePoem.do?poemId=14750 (accessed 7 August 2013).

——— (2007) *We Brits*. Newcastle: Bloodaxe Books Ltd.

——— (2009) *Alternative Anthem: Selected Poems*. Northumberland: Bloodaxe Books Ltd.

——— (2013) *Travel Light, Travel Dark*. Northumberland: Bloodaxe Books Ltd.

Agard, J. and Kitamura, S. (2008) *The Young Inferno*. London: Frances Lincoln.

Allen-Agostini, L. (2013) 'Interview with Christian Campbell in *The Caribbean Review of Books*': http://caribbeanreviewofbooks.com/crb-archive/22-july-2010/i-must-make-trouble-for-the-nation (accessed 15 February 2013).

Alleyne, M. (1985) *A Linguistic Perspective on the Caribbean*. Washington, DC: The Woodrow Wilson International Center for Scholars.

——— (1989) *Roots of Jamaican Culture*. London: Pluto Press.

Anionwu, E. (2006) *Mary Seacole: 1805–1881*. London: University of West London: http://www.maryseacole.com/maryseacole/pages/mary_main.html (accessed 22 March 2013).

Ashcroft, B., Griffiths, G. and Tiffin, H. (1989) *The Empire Writes Back*. London: Routledge.

Atherton, J.S. (2011) 'Learning and Teaching: Experiential Learning': http://www.learningandteaching.info/learning/experience.htm (accessed 14 August 2011).

Baker, T. (2004) '*Goodison's Poetry – Re-visioning Feminist Mythologies*'. Presentation at Staff/Postgraduate Seminar Series, The Department of Literatures in English, the University of the West Indies, Mona.

——— (2005) 'The Poetry of Olive Senior'. Presentation at Staff/Postgraduate Seminar Series, The Department of Literatures in English, the University of the West Indies, Mona.

Baugh, E. (2000) *It Was the Singing*. Toronto: Sandberry Press.

Baugh, E. (ed.) (2007) *Derek Walcott: Selected Poems*. London: Faber.

Baugh, E. (2011) 'Derek Walcott on Being a Caribbean Poet', in Michael Bucknor and Alison Donnell (eds), *The Routledge Companion to Caribbean Literature*. London: Routledge (pp. 93–8).

Beckles, H. (2000) *Inside Slavery: Process and Legacy in the Caribbean Experience*. Kingston: Canoe Press.

Bennett, L. (1966) *Jamaica Labrish*. Kingston, Jamaica: Sangster Press.

Bennett, L. (2005) 'Colonization in Reverse', in *Jamaica Labrish*. Kingston: Sangsters Book Stores Ltd.

Benton, P. (1999) 'Unweaving the Rainbow: Poetry Teaching in the Secondary School I'. *Oxford Review of Education*, 24 (4): 521–31.

——— (2000) 'The Conveyor Belt Curriculum? Poetry Teaching in the Secondary School II'. *Oxford Review of Education*, 26 (1): 81–93.

Berry, J. (1988) *When I Dance*. London: Hamish Hamilton.

——— (2004) 'Childhood Tracks', in *Only One of Me*. London: Pan Macmillan Press.

Bloom, V. (1983) *Touch Mi! Tell Mi!* London: Bogle-L'Ouverture.

——— (2000) *The World Is Sweet*. London: Bloomsbury Children's Books: www.poetryarchive.org/poetryarchive/singlePoem.do?poemId=1693,&lrm (accessed 10 May 2013).

Bonham-Carter, C. (2012) Teaching Caribbean Poetry Course: Final Assignment submitted for the Teaching Caribbean Poetry course, UK (January).

Brathwaite, E. (1973) *The Arrivants: A New World Trilogy – Rights of Passage/Islands/Masks*. Oxford: Oxford University Press.

——— (1974) *Contradictory Omens: Cultural Diversity and Integration in the Caribbean*. Mona: Savacou.

——— (1975) 'Caribbean Man in Space and Time'. *Savacou* 11/12 September, 7.

——— (1984) *History of the Voice: The Development of Nation Language in Anglophone Caribbean Poetry*. London: New Beacon Books.

Brathwaite, K. (1981) *The Arrivants*. Oxford: Oxford University Press.

——— (1994) *Barabajan Poems*. New York: Savacou North.

——— (2005) *Born to Slow Horses*. Middletown, CT: Wesleyan University Press.

Breeze, J. (1992) Spring Cleaning. London: Virago.

Breiner, L. (1998) *An Introduction to West Indian Poetry*. Cambridge: Cambridge University Press.

Brindley, S. (1994) *Teaching English*. London: Routledge.

Britannica Online Encyclopaedia: http://www.britannica.com/EBchecked/topic/625820/veranda (accessed 9 May 2013).

Britton, L. (1984) 'Viewpoints: The Distinction between Participants and Spectator Role in Language Research and Practice'. *Research in the Teaching of English*, 18(3): 320–31.

Brown, S. (2007a) *Tourist, Traveller, Troublemaker: Essays on Poetry*. Leeds: Peepal Tree Press.

——— (2007b) '"Nothing about us at all": Olive Senior and West Indian Poetry', in *Tourist, Traveller, Troublemaker: Essays on Poetry*, pp. 149–155.

Brown, S. and McWatt, M. (2005) *The Oxford Book of Caribbean Verse*. Oxford: Oxford University Press.

Brown, S., Mervyn, M. and Gordon. R. (eds) (1989) *Voiceprint: An Anthology of Oral and Related Poetry from the Caribbean*. Harlow: Longman.

Bryan, B. (1995) 'The Role of Context in Defining Adolescent Responses to Caribbean Poetry'. *English in Education*, 29 (1): 42–9.

——— (1998) 'A Comparison of Approaches to Teaching English in Two Sociolinguistic Environments (Jamaica and London)'. PhD dissertation, Institute of Education, University of London.

——— (2010) *Between Two Grammars: Language Learning and Teaching in a Creole-Speaking Environment*. Kingston: Ian Randle Publications.

——— (2011) *Report on the Teaching Caribbean Poetry Project*, School of Education Report to the Board of the Faculty of Humanities and Education, University of West Indies, Mona.

Bryan, B., Dadzie, S. and Scafe, S. (1985) *Heart of the Race: Black Women's Lives in Britain*. London: Virago Press.

Campbell, C. (2010) *Running the Dusk*. Leeds: Peepal Tree Press.

Carberry, H.D. (1995) 'Nature', in *It Takes a Mighty Fire*. Jamaica: Ian Randle Publishers. zahuren.wordpress.com/poems/nature-by-h-d-carberry/.

Caribbean Secondary Examination (CXC) Reports on English A: 2006, 2008, 2010. CXC, Barbados.

Carter, M. (1989) 'This is the Dark Time, My Love', in Kenneth Ramchand and Cecil Gray (eds), *West Indian Poetry*. Kingston: Carlong Publishers.

——— (1997) *Selected Poems*. Georgetown: Red Thread Women's Press.

Cassidy, F. (1971) *Jamaica Talk: Three Hundred Years of the English Language in Jamaica,* 2nd edn. London: Macmillan Caribbean.

Chamberlain, J. Edward (1993) *Come Back to Me My Language: Poetry and the West Indies.* Chicago: University of Illinois Press.

Christie, P. (2003) *Language in Jamaica.* Kingston: Arawak Publications.

Collins, M. (2003) *Lady In A Boat.* Leeds: Peepal Tree.

Cooke, J. and Thompson, J. (1980) 'Three Poets on the Teaching of Poetry'. *College English,* 42 (2): 133–41.

Dabydeen, D. Review of 'Travel Light Travel Dark' by John Agard: http://www.bloodaxebooks .com/titlepage.asp?isbn=1852249919 (accessed 15 August 2013).

D'Aguiar, F. (1985) *Mama Dot.* London: Chatto Poetry.

——— (2002) 'Introduction', in L. Johnson, *Mi Revalueshanary Fren: Selected Poems.* London: Penguin Books.

Dawes, K. (1999) *Natural Mysticism: Towards a New Reggae Aesthetic.* Leeds: Peepal Tree Press.

——— (2007) 'Writing Home Away from Home', in Mervyn Morris and Carolyn Allen (eds), *Writing Life: Reflections by West Indian Writers.* Kingston: Ian Randle Publishers.

Dawes, K. (2008) *Wheel and Come Again: an Anthology of Reggae Poetry.* Leeds: Peepal Tree Press Ltd.

——— (2009) quoted in Dieffenthaller, I. *Snow on Sugarcane: the Evolution of West Indian Poetry in Britain.* Newcastle-Upon-Tyne: Cambridge Scholars Publishing.

Dawes, K. (ed.) (2010) *Red: Contemporary Black British Poetry.* Leeds: Peepal Tree Press.

Dieffenthaller, I. (2009) *Snow on Sugarcane: The Evolution of West Indian Poetry in Britain.* Newcastle-Upon-Tyne: Cambridge Scholars Publishing.

Donnell, A. (2006) *Twentieth-Century Caribbean Literature: Critical Moments in Anglophone Literary History.* Oxon: Routledge.

Dooley, M. Review of 'Travel Light Travel Dark' by John Agard: http://www.bloodaxebooks. com/titlepage.asp?isbn=1852249919 (accessed 15 August 2013).

Dymoke, S. (2012) 'Poetry is an Unfamiliar Text: Locating Poetry in Secondary Classrooms in New Zealand and England during a Period of Curriculum Change'. *Changing English,* 19: 395–410.

Edwards, V. (1979) *The West Indian Language Issue in British Schools: Challenges and Responses.* London: Routledge.

Eliot, T.S. (1969) 'The Waste Land', in *The Complete Poems and Plays of T.S. Eliot.* London: Faber and Faber.

Garrison, L. (1979) *Black Youth, Rastafarianism and the Identity Crisis in Britain.* London: Afro-Caribbean Education Resource (ACER) Project Publication.

Goodison, L (1992) 'My Will', in *Selected Poems.* Michigan: University of Michigan Press, p. 138.

——— (1993) *Selected Poems.* Michigan: University of Michigan Press.

——— (2002) *Lorna Goodison – Selected Poems.* Michigan: University of Michigan Press.

Gordon, J. (2004) 'Verbal Energy: Attending to Poetry'. *English in Education,* 38: 92–103.

Gordon, S. (1963) *A Century of West Indian Education.* London: Green and Co. Ltd.

Gottlieb, K. (2000) *The Mother of Us All: A History of Queen Nanny.* Trenton: Africa World Press.

Government of Jamaica, National Heroes listing: http://www.jis.gov.jm/special_sections/Heroes/ Heroes1.htm#Nanny (accessed 1 March 2013).

Grossman, P., Hammerness, K. and McDonald, M. (2009) 'Redefining Teacher: Re-imagining Teacher Education'. *Teachers and Teaching: Theory and Practice,* 15(2): 273–90.

Hammerness, K., Darling-Hammond, L. and Bransford, J. with Berliner, D. and Cochran-Smith, M., McDonald, M. and Zeichner, K. (2005) 'How Teachers Learn and Develop', in L. Darling-Hammond and J. Bransford (eds), *Preparing Teachers for a Changing World: What Teachers Should Learn and Be Able to Do.* San Francisco, CA: Jossey-Bass, pp. 359–89.

Jarrett-Macauley, D. (1998) *The Life of Una Marson.* Manchester: Manchester University Press.

Johnson, L.K. (1974) *Voices of the Living and the Dead.* London: Race Today Publications.

—— (1978) *Dread, Beat and Blood*. Place: Frontline Label.

—— (1980) *Inglan Is a Bitch*. London: Race Today Publications.

—— (2002) *Mi Revalueshanary Fren: Selected Poems*. London: Penguin Books.

—— (2007a) Remembering Mikey Smith, in A. Paul (ed.), *Caribbean Culture*. Kingston: UWI Press.

—— (2007b) *Selected Poems*. London: Penguin Books.

Joseph, A. (2011) *Rubber Orchestras*. Norfolk: Salt Publishing.

—— (2012) *Bird Head Son*. Norfolk: Salt Publishing.

Kincaid, J. (1988) *A Small Place*. London: Virago Press.

Kraidy, M. (2005) *Hybridity, or the Cultural Logic of Globalization*. Philadelphia, PA: Temple University Press.

Levy, A. (2004) *Small Island*. London: Picador.

—— (2011) *The Long Song*. London: Headline Review.

Lovelace, E. (2011) Review of 'Rubber Orchestras' by Anthony Joseph: http://www.fishpond.com.au/Books/Rubber-Orchestras-Anthony-Joseph/9781844718191 (accessed 7 August 2013).

Makoni, S., Smitherman, G., Ball, A. and Spears, K. (2003) *Black Linguistics: Language, Society, and Politics in Africa and the Americas*. London: Routledge.

Marson, U. (1937) 'Kinky Hair Blues': http://www.scrapbook.com/poems/doc/30737/141.html (accessed 7 July 2012).

McDonald, I. and Brown, S. (eds) (1992) *The Heinemann Book of Caribbean Poetry*. Oxford: Heinemann Educational Publishers.

McGill, R. (2003) 'Goon Poets of the Black Atlantic: Linton Kwesi Johnson's Imagined Canon'. *Textual Practice*, 17 (3): 561–74.

—— (2000) *Voices of the Other: Children's Literature and the Postcolonial Context*. New York: Routledge.

McKay, C. (1992) 'Two-An'-Six': http://www.poemhunter.com/poem/two-an-six/ (accessed 9 June 2012).

McNeal, J. and Rogers, M. (eds) (1971) *The Multi-racial School: A Professional Perspective*. Harmondsworth: Penguin Books.

Miller, K. (2007) *There Is an Anger that Moves*. Manchester: Carcanet Press.

—— (2010) 'Twelve Notes for a Light Song of Light', in *A Light Song of Light*. Manchester: Caranet Press Ltd, pp. 11–16.

Morris, M. (1999) *Is English We Speaking*. Jamaica: Ian Randle Publishers.

—— (2005) *Making West Indian Literature*. Kingston: Ian Randle Publishers.

—— (2006) *I Been There, Sort Of*. Manchester: Carcanet Press.

Morris, M. and Allen, C. (eds) (2007) *Writing Life: Reflections by West Indian Writers*. Kingston: Ian Randle Publishers.

Naidoo, B. (ed.) (1992) *Free as I Know*. London: Harper Collins Educational.

Nichols, G. (1983) *I Is a Long-Memoried Woman*. Caribbean Cultural International. Austin, TX: University of Texas Press.

—— (1984) *The Fat Black Woman's Poems*. London: Virago Press.

—— (1988a) *Come On Into My Tropical Garden*. London: Bloomsbury.

—— (1988b) in M. Styles and H. Cook (eds), *There's a Poet Behind You*. London: A&C Black, pp. 6–23.

—— (1989) *Lazy Thoughts of a Lazy Woman*. London: Virago Press Ltd.

—— (2010) *I Have Crossed an Ocean: Selected Poems*. Newcastle: Bloodaxe Books.

—— (1990) *An Integrated Language Perspective in the Elementary School*. Longman: New York.

Parker, M. (2011) *The Sugar Barons*. London: Hutchinson.

Philip, M. NourbeSe. (2005) 'Oliver Twist', in *The Penguin Book of Caribbean Verse In English*. London: Penguin.

Philip, M. NourbeSe (2008) *Zong!* Middletown, CT: Wesleyan University Press.

Pollard,V. (ed.) (1980) *Nine West Indian Poets: An anthology for the CXC Examination*. London: Collins.

Pollard, V. (1988) *Crown Point and Other Poems*. Leeds: Peepal Tree Press

—— (1992) *Shame Trees Don't Grow Here*. Leeds: Peepal Tree Press.

—— (1993) *From Jamaican Creole to Standard English: A Handbook for Jamaican Teachers*. New York: Caribbean Research Center, Medgar Evers College.

—— (1994) *Dread Talk: The Language of Rastafari*. Mona: University of the West Indies Press.

—— (2005) 'Beware the Naked Man Who Offers You a Shirt', in *The Penguin Book of Caribbean Verse In English*. London: Penguin.

—— (2009) *Leaving Traces*. Leeds: Peepal Tree Press.

Rampton, B. (1995) *Crossing: Language and Ethnicity among Adolescents*. London: Longman.

Reynolds, K. (2007) *Radical Children's Literature: Future Visions and Aesthetic Transformations in Juvenile Fiction*. New York: Palgrave MacMillan.

Roach, E. (1992) 'Love Overgrows a Rock', in *The Flowering Rock: Collected Poems, 1938–74*. Leeds: Peepal Tree Press Ltd.

Roberts, P. (1997) *From Oral to Literate Culture: Colonial Experiences in the English West Indies*. Kingston: University of the West Indies Press.

Rohlehr, G. (1970) 'Sparrow and the Language of Calypso'. *Savacou* 2. 87–99.

—— (1992) 'The Problem of the Problem of Form', in *The Shape of that Hurt, and Other Essays*. Port of Spain: Longman, pp. 1–65.

—— (2004) *A Scuffling of Islands: Essays on Calypso*. Port of Spain: Lexicon Trinidad Ltd.

Rosenblatt, L. (1991) 'Literary Theory', in J. Flood, J. Jensen, D. Lapp and J. Squire (eds), *Handbook of Research on Teaching the English Language Arts*. New York: Macmillan, pp. 57–62.

Scafe, S. (1989) *Teaching Black Literature*. London: Virago.

Scott, D. (1973) *Uncle Time*. Pittsburgh, PA: University of Pittsburgh Press.

—— (1982) *Dreadwalk*. London: New Beacon Books

Senior, O. (1985) 'Colonial Girls School', in *Talking of Trees*. Kingston, Jamaica: Calabash: http://www.poetryarchive.org/poetryarchive/singlePoem.do?poemId=14917 (accessed 7 August 2013).

—— (2003) *Encyclopedia of Jamaican Heritage*. Kingston: Twin Guinep Publishers.

—— (2005) 'Meditation on Yellow', in *Gardening in the Tropics*. Toronto: Insomniac Press. First published McClelland and Stewart, 1994, pp. 11–18; Bloodaxe Books, 1995.

Sherlock, P. and Bennett, H. (1998) *The Story of the Jamaican People*. Kingston: Ian Randle Publishers.

Shirley, T. (2009) *She Who Sleeps With Bones*. Leeds: Peepal Tree Press.

Showalter, E. (2003) *Teaching Literature*. Oxford: Blackwell Publishing.

Sidney, P. (1915, first published 1595) *An Apologie for Poetrie*. Edited by E.S. Shuckburgh. Cambridge: Cambridge University Press.

Smartt, D. (2001) *Connecting Medium*. Leeds: Peepal Tree Press.

—— (2008) *Ship Shape*. Leeds: Peepal Tree Press.

Stewart, R. (1993) 'Linton Kwesi Johnson: Poetry Down a Reggae Wire'. *New West Indian Guide* 67 (1/2): 69–89.

Stone, M. (1981) *The Mis-education of the Black Child*. London: Fontana.

Styles, M. (1998) *From the Garden to the Street*. London: Cassell.

Styles, M. and Cook, H. (eds) (1988) *There's a Poet Behind You . . .* London: A & C Black.

Sumara, D. (2002) *Why Reading Literature in School Still Matters: Imagination, Interpretation, Insight*. Mahwah, NJ: Lawrence Erlbaum Associates.

U Tam'si, T. (1972) *Selected Poems*. London: Heinemann Educational.

Walcott, D. (1969a) *In A Green Night,* London: Jonathan Cape.

—— (1969b) *The Castaway,* London: Jonathan Cape.

—— (1973) *Another Life,* London: Jonathan Cape.

———— (1976) *Sea Grapes*, London: Jonathan Cape.

———— (1980) *The Star-Apple Kingdom,* London: Jonathan Cape.

———— (1981) 'The Spoiler's Return', in *The Fortunate Traveller.* New York: Farrar Straus Giroux, pp. 53–60.

———— (1982) *The Fortunate Traveller,* London: Faber and Faber.

———— (1987) *Collected Poems 1948–1984.* New York: Farrar, Straus and Giroux.

———— (1988, first published 1987) *The Arkansas Testament,* London: Faber and Faber.

———— (1998) 'The Antilles: Fragments of Epic Memory', in *What the Twilight Says.* New York: Farrar, Straus and Giroux, pp. 65–84.

———— (2007) 'The Light of the World', in *Selected Poems.* New York: Farrar, Straus and Giroux, pp. 184–7.

Ware, T. (2012) 'Teaching Caribbean Poetry Course: Final Assignment'. Paper presented on the Cambridge poetry course. January 2012.

Warner, M. (1999) *Trinidad Yoruba: From Mother Tongue To Memory.* Mona: The University of the West Indies Press.

Williams, E. (1994) *Capitalism and Slavery.* Charlotte, NC: University of North Carolina Press.

Young, Robert J.C. (2003) *Postcolonialism: A Very Short Introduction.* Oxford: OUP.

Zephaniah, B. (1996a) *Propa Propaganda.* London: Bloodaxe Books.

———— (1996b) *Funky Chickens.* London: Viking.

———— (1997) *Funky Chickens.* London: Penguin Group.

Index